T0364146

The Political Economy of
Trade Protection

A National Bureau
of Economic Research
Project Report

The Political Economy of Trade Protection

Edited by Anne O. Krueger

The University of Chicago Press

Chicago and London

ANNE O. KRUEGER is professor of economics at Stanford University and a research associate of the National Bureau of Economic Research.

The University of Chicago Press, Chicago 60637
The University of Chicago Press, Ltd., London
© 1996 by The National Bureau of Economic Research
All rights reserved. Published 1996
Printed in the United States of America
05 04 03 02 01 00 99 98 97 96   1 2 3 4 5
ISBN: 0-226-45491-6 (cloth)

Library of Congress Cataloging-in-Publication Data

The Political economy of trade protection / edited by Anne O. Krueger.
          p.   cm.—(A National Bureau of Economic Research project report)
    Papers presented at a one-day conference in Washington, DC, sponsored by the National Bureau of Economic Research.
    Includes bibliographical references and index.
    1. United States—Commercial policy—Congresses.   2. Free trade—United States—Congresses.   3. Foreign trade regulation—United States—Congresses.   4. Protectionism—Congresses.   5. Antidumping duties—Congresses.   I. Krueger, Anne O.   II. Series.
HF1455.P544   1996
382'.7'0973—dc20   95-4789
                                                                        CIP

⊗ The paper used in this publication meets the minimum requirements of the American National Standard for Information Sciences—Permanence of Paper for Printed Library Materials, ANSI Z39.48-1984.

Relation of the Directors to the
Work and Publications of the
National Bureau of Economic Research

1. The object of the National Bureau of Economic Research is to ascertain and to present to the public important economic facts and their interpretation in a scientific and impartial manner. The board of Directors is charged with the responsibility of ensuring that the work of the National Bureau is carried on in strict conformity with this object.

2. The President of the National Bureau shall submit to the Board of Directors, or to its Executive Committee, for their formal adoption all specific proposals for research to be instituted.

3. No research report shall be published by the National Bureau until the President has sent each member of the Board a notice that a manuscript is recommended for publication and that in the President's opinion it is suitable for publication in accordance with the principles of the National Bureau. Such notification will include an abstract or summary of the manuscript's content and a response form for use by those Directors who desire a copy of the manuscript for review. Each manuscript shall contain a summary drawing attention to the nature and treatment of the problem studied, the character of the data and their utilization in the report, and the main conclusions reached.

4. For each manuscript so submitted, a special committee of the Directors (including Directors Emeriti) shall be appointed by majority agreement of the President and Vice Presidents (or by the Executive Committee in case of inability to decide on the part of the President and Vice Presidents), consisting of three Directors selected as nearly as may be one from each general division of the Board. The names of the special manuscript committee shall be stated to each Director when notice of the proposed publication is submitted to him. It shall be the duty of each member of the special manuscript committee to read the manuscript. If each member of the manuscript committee signifies his approval within thirty days of the transmittal of the manuscript, the report may be published. If at the end of that period any member of the manuscript committee withholds his approval, the President shall then notify each member of the Board, requesting approval or disapproval of publication, and thirty days additional shall be granted for this purpose. The manuscript shall then not be published unless at least a majority of the entire Board who shall have voted on the proposal within the time fixed for the receipt of votes shall have approved.

5. No manuscript may be published, though approved by each member of the special manuscript committee, until forty-five days have elapsed from the transmittal of the report in manuscript form. The interval is allowed for the receipt of any memorandum of dissent or reservation, together with a brief statement of his reasons, that any member may wish to express; and such memorandum of dissent or reservation shall be published with the manuscript if he so desires. Publication does not, however, imply that each member of the Board has read the manuscript, or that either members of the Board in general or the special committee have passed on its validity in every detail.

6. Publications of the National Bureau issued for informational purposes concerning the work of the Bureau and its staff, or issued to inform the public of activities of Bureau staff, and volumes issued as a result of various conferences involving the National Bureau shall contain a specific disclaimer noting that such publication has not passed through the normal review procedures required in this resolution. The Executive Committee of the Board is charged with review of all such publications from time to time to ensure that they do not take on the character of formal research reports of the National Bureau, requiring formal Board approval.

7. Unless otherwise determined by the Board or exempted by the terms of paragraph 6, a copy of this resolution shall be printed in each National Bureau publication.

(Resolution adopted October 25, 1926, as revised through September 30, 1974)

Contents

Acknowledgments

The papers contained in this volume were presented at a one-day conference in Washington, D.C., sponsored by the National Bureau of Economic Research. It was intended that the results of a large research project be made readily accessible to a wider audience than would read the full research project results. The full results were presented at an earlier conference held in Cambridge, Massachusetts, and will be published in a separate volume.

The research underlying the papers in this volume had been undertaken in an NBER-sponsored project on the political economy of trade protection, financed by the Ford Foundation. The editor and the authors of individual papers are grateful to the Ford Foundation for its support, and especially to Seamus O'Clearicain for his interest in the project.

The editor thanks all the authors and discussants in the original project for their contributions. A special thanks is due to all of the contributors to this volume for their willingness to undertake yet another task once the original project had been completed. Martin Feldstein was instrumental in supporting the project throughout, and especially in encouraging this volume. In addition, Kirsten Foss Davis was her usual efficient self in organizing the Washington conference, and Deborah Kiernan has been invaluable in seeing the conference papers through to publication.

Introduction

Anne O. Krueger

One of the central tenets of economists for the past two centuries has been the proposition that free trade between nations will in most circumstances be highly beneficial, and that any nation which unilaterally adopts a policy of free trade will benefit.[1] There are exceptions to the argument for free trade, such as in cases of infant industries and more recently "the new trade theory."[2]

Nonetheless, it has been a source of considerable frustration to most international economists that, in reality, protection to industries, and pressure for it, is granted in circumstances that appear to bear little resemblance to those cases in which economic analysis suggests it might be warranted on the grounds of national economic interest.

Many have therefore turned their attention to attempting to understand the "political economy" of protection, by which is meant the actual determinants of which industries receive protection, and of the structure of protection across industries.

Most such efforts have focused on the empirical estimation of models in

Anne O. Krueger is professor of economics at Stanford University and a research associate of the National Bureau of Economic Research.

1. The recognized exception to this generalization that is relevant for the United States is when a country has monopoly power in trade. Even that exception, however, is contingent upon the trading partners being unable to retaliate in ways that are sufficiently harmful. There are also arguments that "market failures," such an externalities, might make the adoption of a free-trade policy less desirable. Economists' standard answer to that, however, has been to note that the appropriate policy response to these failures is to correct them at their source, i.e., to impose a tax or subsidy to reflect the value of the externality.

2. The "new" trade theory demonstrates that there *may* be circumstances under which an intervention in trade (which might be an export subsidy, an export tax, an import duty, or even an import subsidy) could increase the total economic well-being of a country in circumstances where the first entrant(s) to an industry become established and receive the economic rents that accrue to first-comers. The rationale is that first entrants can achieve a scale of production sufficient enough to simultaneously charge a low enough price to deter other entrants and still have that price significantly above the marginal cost of production.

which the presence of tariffs (or other trade barriers) and/or their height is to be explained. Variables such as the level of employment in the industry, the trend in the industry's employment and profitability, and the geographic concentration of the industry are then used as possible explanatory factors. In general, almost every variable appeared to have explanatory power in some cases, but there was no strong systematic pattern that emerged from these analyses.

The National Bureau of Economic Research project on the political economy of U.S. trade policy was designed to try to supplement and enrich the understanding of the political economy of trade policy by undertaking parallel analyses of the determinants of protection and its evolution in a number of American industries (seven, in the event), and by examining the determinants of administered protection across industries.[3] The hope was that in-depth investigations of how protection actually has evolved in industries whose circumstances were evidently dissimilar would shed light on the process of protection and its determinants, and perhaps yield richer hypotheses for further analysis.

The industries chosen for inclusion are textiles and apparel (the Multi-Fibre Arrangement [MFA]), steel, automobiles, semiconductors, lumber, wheat, and agricultural protection as negotiated under the North American Free Trade Agreement (NAFTA). These analyses were supplemented by a "cross-section" study of determinants of "administered protection."

Textiles and apparel represent an industry whose fortunes have been declining since the early part of the twentieth century, and where pressures for protection have been intense since the mid-1950s. Many parts of the industry are relatively labor-intensive, and it is geographically widespread. Protection has been granted to the industry under the Multi-Fibre Arrangement, an increasingly complex set of quantitative restrictions on imports negotiated by individual product category under an umbrella arrangement concluded under the auspices of the General Agreement on Tariffs and Trade (GATT).[4] Steel and automobiles, by contrast, are industries in which U.S. firms held dominant positions worldwide until at least the early 1970s. Since that time, both industries have lost their preeminent positions, imports have increased, and both have sought protection. Both are highly visible industries but neither is labor-intensive, and both are reasonably geographically concentrated. Protection for automobiles came in the form of voluntary export restraints (VERs) on imports from Japan during the early and mid-1980s—although there had been pressures earlier, only then were VERs adopted and later abandoned. Protection for steel under VERs and other administrative arrangements was accorded for much of the 1970s and 1980s after the industry filed a large number of complaints alleging unfair trade practices on the part of foreign producers. These

---

3. "Administered protection" is the term applied to the use of the countervailing duty (against foreign subsidies) and antidumping (against pricing below cost or below sales price in other markets) administrative law by firms seeking relief from import competition.

4. Under the Uruguay Round agreement, the MFA is to be phased out over a twelve-year period.

pending cases were then used as a bargaining instrument in negotiating export restraints with foreign governments. By the end of the 1980s, however, the steel industry's ability to achieve protection through this means was greatly diminished.

The semiconductor industry, by contrast, is much smaller and is also a "new" industry. It is certainly not labor-intensive, and it is reasonably geographically concentrated. Its initial development in the 1960s and 1970s was led by American firms, but by the late 1970s the preeminence of these firms was being challenged by a successful Japanese entry into the market. Starting in the early 1980s it sought protection, which it finally achieved, at least in part, in the Semiconductor Agreement of 1986 and subsequent agreements negotiated with Japan.

Interestingly, these four industries were protected through bilateral arrangements made by the United States and foreign governments. As can be seen in the individual studies in this volume, the U.S. administration (and the foreign government) was frequently reluctant to enter into such protective arrangements but did so in the belief that failure to undertake these measures would spur "administered protection" or congressional action that might be even more protective of the industry.

The U.S. lumber industry represents yet another situation. The industry is relatively small and geographically concentrated. It certainly does not have the visibility of textiles and apparel, steel, automobiles, or even semiconductors. Nonetheless, since the early 1980s, the U.S. lumber industry has also sought protection against Canadian imports through the administered protection process. In the eyes of many U.S. trading partners and economists, administered protection under U.S. trade laws has become the "protectionist weapon of choice." As such, inclusion of an industry whose primary approach to the protection process was through the use of fair trade laws seemed highly desirable in the project.

The final two studies focus on agriculture, where the mechanisms and instruments used for protection are quite different from those of American industry. One focuses on wheat. Wheat has long been a major grain crop in the Midwest, one in which the United States is generally believed to have considerable comparative advantage. An export enhancement program for wheat, under which American wheat farmers in effect received protection in their exports during the 1980s, provided considerable protection to American wheat exports.

The other agricultural study examines the rule and fortunes of various agricultural groups in the negotiations leading up to NAFTA. Some producer groups were considerably more effective than others in delaying the time or reducing the rate at which trade with Mexico would be freed from restraints. An analysis of who was influential, and why, sheds further light on the determinants of protection.

The final study focuses on administered protection seen from a different perspective. Critics of U.S. trade law (antidumping and countervailing duty legislation) have suggested that the very processes that are established confer protection to U.S. industries, regardless of whether the outcome of the process finds for the complainant and grants protection. Robert Staiger and Frank Wolak study this phenomenon, with findings that are important in their own right, and simultaneously provide insight from yet another angle into the overall political economy of protection.

Each study can stand alone. But together they shed additional light on the political economy of U.S. trade policies. The first seven chapters examine the studies individually. A final chapter then summarizes some of the important questions that arise, from a policy perspective, from the findings in the individual studies. Much more complete analyses of the individual cases and the findings can be found in the NBER volume based on the project that is forthcoming from the University of Chicago Press, *The Political Economy of American Trade Policy.*

1 The U.S.-Japan Semiconductor Trade Conflict

Douglas A. Irwin

1.1 Introduction

The 1986 U.S.-Japan semiconductor trade agreement ranks among the most controversial trade policy actions of the 1980s. In this agreement the government of Japan agreed to end the "dumping" of semiconductors in world markets (not just the United States) and to help secure 20 percent of their domestic semiconductor market for foreign producers within five years.

The antidumping provisions—resulting in part from the extraordinary self-initiation of an antidumping action by the U.S. government—later proved to be partly illegal under the General Agreement on Tariffs and Trade (GATT) and drew the ire of prominent high-technology, semiconductor-using industries, particularly computer manufacturers. Computer producers formed a countervailing interest group to oppose these provisions and eventually forced them to be dropped in the 1991 renegotiation of the agreement.

The 20 percent market share provision—an exceptional request from the standpoint of traditional U.S. trade policy—was the negotiated solution to the problem of market access in Japan based on circumstantial evidence that the market was closed to foreign semiconductor producers. These producers did achieve a 20.2 percent market share in Japan by the end of 1992, although the share has subsequently fluctuated. But by concentrating on a specific, quantitative "outcome" rather than the principle of market access, the provision provoked sharp debate: either it was heralded as a positive, concrete step toward gaining greater sales in Japan ("making the cash registers ring") or

Douglas A. Irwin is associate professor of business economics at the Graduate School of Business at the University of Chicago and a faculty research associate of the National Bureau of Economic Research. He served on the staff of the President's Council of Economic Advisers from 1986 to 1987.

scorned as a step toward cartelized "managed trade" and export protectionism via government-fixed market shares.[1]

Few industries ever receive the sustained, high-level attention needed to result in the negotiation of a governmental agreement on trade in just one sector. This paper examines how the U.S. semiconductor industry became the beneficiary of this unprecedented sectoral trade agreement.[2]

1.2   The U.S. Semiconductor Industry

The U.S. semiconductor industry—a prominent, high-technology, R&D-intensive industry—produced $25 billion in output with employment of just under 200,000 in 1989.

1.2.1   Firms

Firms range from the enormous—such as IBM, the world's largest semiconductor producer in the mid-1980s—to the minuscule—such as Micron Technology of Boise, Idaho, which specialized in memory chips. Although Micron's sales were only $2/10$ of 1 percent of IBM's, both firms equally influenced the course of U.S. trade policy. Between these extremes lie a handful of prominent midsized firms that constitute the core of the U.S. industry: Texas Instruments (TI), Motorola, Advanced Micro Devices (AMD), National Semiconductor, and Intel.

1.2.2   Products

The 1980s trade dispute centered on a unique set of digital integrated circuits—memory chips—which computers use to store and retrieve data and which accounted for 18 percent of all U.S. semiconductor purchases in 1985. Dynamic random-access memories (DRAMs) comprised 7 percent of the total market. The DRAM market approaches perfect competition because DRAMs are a standardized commodity produced by many firms.[3]

1.2.3   Capital and Labor

In 1977 corporate executives, the principal capital owners in the industry (many firms were still dominated by their founders), formed the Semiconductor Industry Association (SIA) to lobby for trade actions. Some firms organized political action committees, whose disbursements appear related to the trade

1. The Clinton administration has promised to use import targets with Japan in other sectors. For a critical analysis, see Irwin (1994).

2. This paper is a significantly condensed version of my longer paper of the same title issued as NBER Working Paper no. 4745, May 1994. The longer version should be consulted for fuller details of this issue.

3. The industry is often thought to be a strategic industry because of learning spillovers. For an assessment, see Irwin and Klenow (1994).

dispute with Japan.[4] With one-third of U.S. semiconductor employment in California, the SIA ably employed California's congressional representatives to pressure the executive branch into trade action.

Labor itself was largely mute. The lack of political activism among workers could be attributed to their interindustry mobility: evidence suggests that many of them have skills useful in related high-technology industries.[5]

1.2.4   Merchants and Captives

Captive producers, such as IBM and AT&T, are vertically integrated (making semiconductors for internal consumption) but are net purchasers of semiconductors from others. Merchant firms produce semiconductors for sale to other firms. Merchant firms have an interest in high semiconductor prices, whereas captive producers do not. These conflicting interests within the SIA had to partially accommodate each other.

1.2.5   Downstream Users

Computer manufacturers are the most important domestic users of memory chips and could be expected to oppose proposals that would raise semiconductor prices. These manufacturers did not initially oppose the 1986 agreement, but did so with the subsequent rise in DRAM prices.

1.2.6   Japanese Producers

Japanese lobbying during the antidumping and Section 301 (of the Trade Act of 1974) deliberations was limited because of the strict administrative procedures under U.S. trade law. The Electronic Industries Association of Japan (EIAJ) and its members spent $3.8 million on K Street lawyers for their legal defense between 1985 and 1987.[6]

1.3   Semiconductor Competition from Japan

Japan emerged as a major producer of semiconductors in the late 1970s. Spectacular success was achieved in DRAMs: the U.S. market share plummeted from 70 to 20 percent between 1978 and 1986 as the Japanese share jumped from under 30 to about 75 percent.[7] Import penetration increased. Japan's share of total U.S. semiconductor consumption rose from 7.5 percent in 1982 to 12.3 percent in 1984, before dropping back to 9.8 percent in 1986. Yet

---

4. According to the Federal Election Commission, payments totaled $354,318 at the peak of the dispute in 1985 and 1986, 40 percent higher than in 1983 and 1984.

5. See Ong and Mar (1992).

6. Roughly $1.1 million over these three years was devoted to countering the Section 301 action, comparable to that spent by the SIA alone on the Section 301 case. Figures from the Department of Justice.

7. See Tyson (1992, 106 ff).

Japan's share of the U.S. market was not fully indicative of the force of the new competition because, in an integrated world market, Japanese producers could capture market share abroad only by forcing the market price downward everywhere.

Why were Japanese firms so successful? The role of the Ministry of International Trade and Industry (MITI) and industrial policy has been wholly exaggerated by those sympathetic to the semiconductor industry. Japanese firms probably had easier access to capital: they are often affiliated with a large bank that could play a role in corporate governance through equity ownership (the Glass-Steagall Act prohibits such activities in the United States). Such bank ties probably allowed Japanese producers to weather industry downturns much better than their U.S. counterparts.[8] On the U.S. side, the high cost of capital in the early 1980s, the appreciation of the U.S. dollar, lagging adoption of new process technology, and quality control problems all hampered U.S. firms.

1.4   Trade Action against Japan

SIA members had two complaints about their foreign rivals: dumping and market access.

1.4.1   Dumping

The dumping complaints arose during the periodic sharp price declines in this cyclically volatile industry. The industry recession of 1985 was extremely severe because of a brief slowdown in the computer market. After increasing by a factor of five between 1981 and 1984, domestic shipments of microcomputers actually fell by 8 percent in 1985.

Prices collapsed and the memory-chip market contracted 60 percent. Merchant firms racked up unprecedented losses. Capacity utilization and employment plummeted. Every U.S. merchant producer was pushed out of the DRAM market except Texas Instruments and Micron.[9]

Despite complaints that dumping was "predatory" and "unfair," Japan did not pick 1985 as the year to drive U.S. firms out of business. Indeed, Japanese firms experienced similar losses and layoffs as world demand fell. Imports did not cause the recession: Japanese import penetration actually fell in the two years after 1984. Three-quarters of the fall in revenues of U.S.-based companies in 1985 were due to declining overall demand, only a quarter due to lost market share.[10]

Regardless of the underlying economics, the antidumping laws were always available. Captive producers opposed higher tariffs on semiconductors and prevented the SIA from ever filing an antidumping complaint. A small firm that

8. See Hoshi, Kashyap, and Scharfstein (1990).
9. Most firms simply abandoned DRAM production and concentrated on other product lines, but one (Mostek) went bankrupt in 1985.
10. Federal Interagency Staff Working Group (1987, 10).

at the time was not even a member of the SIA forced the issue. In June 1985, Micron filed an antidumping complaint against Japanese exporters of 64K DRAMs. Merchant SIA members soon broke ranks: in September 1985, Intel, AMD, and National Semiconductor filed for antidumping action against imports of erasable programmable read-only memories (EPROMs) from Japan.[11] In an unusual move, the Commerce Department self-initiated an antidumping case on 256K and future generations of DRAMs in December 1985.

As the petitions ground through the administrative trade bureaucracy, preliminary determinations from the International Trade Commission indicated support for the industry, and final affirmative findings appeared to be inevitable.

1.4.2   Market Access

An important barrier to the sale of foreign semiconductors in Japan was the high degree of vertical integration there (that is, captive production, like IBM and AT&T).[12] Few governmental barriers remained after Japan formally liberalized its semiconductor trade in 1975. The SIA viewed this as a sham because the U.S. share of the Japanese market scarcely budged.

In June 1985, the SIA filed a Section 301 petition with the Office of the United States Trade Representative (USTR), providing circumstantial evidence of market barriers in Japan. In 1984, U.S. producers accounted for over 83 percent of sales in the United States, 55 percent in Europe, 47 percent in elsewhere, yet just 11 percent in Japan. But they had no smoking gun: the strongest statement the SIA could muster was that "these trade [market share] figures, coupled with Japan's protectionist heritage in microelectronics, *strongly suggests* that market barriers still exist in Japan."[13] The SIA demanded "affirmative action" in the Japanese market.

Coincidentally, the SIA's political timing was superb. Unlike in 1982, when a trial Section 301 petition was shot down by USTR William Brock, the massive trade deficit focused the Reagan administration's attention on such matters. The USTR self-initiated Section 301 cases to divert protectionist pressure from closing the U.S. market to opening up foreign markets. The audience for this "tough" trade policy was Congress.[14] With this political backdrop, the SIA's petition was attractive in many respects: it was in line with the administration's emerging stress on opening foreign markets, did not directly advocate closing the U.S. market, and would help mollify congressional critics who wanted a tougher Japan policy.

11. Notably absent from this list was Texas Instruments, the largest U.S. producer of EPROMs with direct investments in Japan.

12. Japanese firms also tended to specialize in certain types of semiconductors and trade these devices with one another based on long-term contracts or long-standing ties to one another.

13. SIA and Dewey Ballantine (1984, 2), emphasis added.

14. The administration desperately sought to avoid a congressional trade bill forcing the president to impose sanctions against countries running a trade surplus with the United States. For a discussion of the political environment of trade policy in the mid-1980s, see Destler (1992).

But any petition guaranteed to generate a major confrontation with Japan would encounter some opposition within the administration. The SIA made vague claims about how Japan's government fostered "Buy Japan" attitudes and identified Japan's market structure (reciprocal trading relationships among firms) as a trade barrier. But what were the explicit government policies that were actionable under Section 301? To some administration officials, past government policies, vertical integration, and long-term relationships hardly seemed to constitute actionable "unfair trade practices."

As for the widely distributed SIA pie charts showing country shares in regional markets, an alternative hypothesis was consistent with no Japanese "unfair" practices: U.S. producers dominated the U.S. market, Japanese producers dominated the Japanese market, and U.S. producers essentially split other markets with other producers, holding a slightly higher share in Europe owing to long-standing direct investments in Europe behind the tariff barrier that kept out Japanese imports. Japanese access to the U.S. market also may have been hindered by discrimination in the distribution system.[15]

But there being no major opponents to the petition, the USTR initiated the Section 301 case against Japan.

1.5   The Semiconductor Trade Agreement of 1986

With the exception of Micron, virtually no party had an interest in seeing the antidumping duties imposed. For captive producers and downstream users, the U.S. market would become a "high-priced island." For merchants, the antidumping remedy alone would still permit Japanese dumping in third markets and kill U.S. sales there. For the Japanese producers, a voluntary export restraint to capture scarcity rents would be preferable to antidumping duties. All forces were driving toward a negotiated settlement before the antidumping duties went into effect.

The negotiations got stuck on third-country dumping and market access. Japan wanted to hedge on both points. The SIA was adamant. Japan capitulated to avoid the automatic imposition of antidumping penalties and possible 301 sanctions. In doing so, the EIAJ felt abandoned by MITI, perhaps accounting for its later reluctance to adhere to guidelines enforcing the agreement.

Japan agreed to take actions that would end dumping in the United States.[16] The agreement on preventing third-market dumping was more vague and the

---

15. U.S. semiconductor firms limited Japanese access by terminating contracts with distributors who agreed to carry Japanese products. Japanese semiconductor firms had only one nationwide distributor in the United States (Marshall Industries) because of the "unspoken ban on Japanese franchises" and the "dictum that large houses will not take on the Japanese so long as they are supported by domestic suppliers." See *Electronic News,* 9 December 1985, S28.

16. The Department of Commerce would determine company-specific price floors each quarter and convey this information to the Japanese firms.

government's obligation less clear. On market access, the agreement exhorted Japanese producers to create more sales opportunities for others. But a secret side-letter explicitly but ambiguously mentioned the 20 percent market share: "the Government of Japan recognizes the U.S. semiconductor industry's expectation" that sales will rise to "slightly above 20 percent" in five years and that "the Government of Japan considers that this can be realized."

What policy measures and instruments did Japan have, beyond mere exhortation, to enforce the agreement and guarantee that Japanese firms did not dump in the world market and bought the requisite amount of foreign-made chips? Implementation, quite mistakenly, was not viewed as a major concern for U.S. negotiators, but it was a real problem for Japan since they did not directly control the industry.

To prevent worldwide dumping, MITI did the only thing it knew how to do—reduce the quantity of semiconductors exported to raise export prices. MITI essentially imposed an "antidumping" voluntary export restraint (VER)—an export restraint designed to meet a price target rather than a quantitative target. MITI issued directives to reduce output but had no statutory authority to force any firm to comply and indeed had difficulty in getting firms to comply.[17] On market access, MITI undertook surveys of firms's purchasing plans and encouraged greater purchases of foreign semiconductors. Once again, they had no direct policy instrument to enforce the provisions and compliance was initially weak.

MITI's inability to bring Japanese firms quickly in line looked like waffling to the SIA and the administration. Fearing Capitol Hill's reaction to another "failed" trade agreement with Japan, President Reagan imposed 100 percent tariffs on $300 million worth of Japanese imports in April 1987. The retaliation ranks among the most dramatic events of postwar U.S. trade policy. Japan was stunned, but some reports indicated that MITI was secretly pleased because it proved to Japanese firms that they should follow MITI's directives.

1.6   Economic Effects of the 1986 Agreement

As with other VERs, the beneficiaries included Japanese exporters. The MITI-induced production cutbacks generated an enormous windfall for exporters. According to some reports, profits on 1M DRAM sales for Japanese producers amounted to $1.2 billion in 1988 alone, which could be plowed back into R&D and product upgrading. Higher DRAM prices accelerated the entry of South Korean firms not covered by the restraint.

Only two U.S. merchant firms (TI and Micron) remained in the DRAM market to benefit from the antidumping actions. DRAM sales reportedly accounted

---

17. However, bureaucratic delays in approval of export licenses—also tightened to prevent dumping—could "unexpectedly" arise for recalcitrant firms.

for as much as 60 percent of TI's profits in 1988 and Micron's sales rose by a factor of six between 1986 and 1988.[18] U.S. producers did not reenter the DRAM market. Motorola agreed to buy prefabricated semiconductor dies from Toshiba, assemble them in Malaysia, and import them under Motorola's name to avoid the antidumping duties. U.S. Memories, a consortium to establish greater domestic DRAM production, was stillborn.

The clear losers from the agreement were semiconductor users, particularly computer manufacturers dependent on DRAMs. They soon fought back.

1.7   Aftermath of the 1986 Agreement

Of the three major provisions of the 1986 agreement, only one (on market access) survived through the renegotiation of the agreement in 1991.

The third-market dumping provision died in 1988. Responding to a complaint from the European Community, a GATT panel ruled that Japanese monitoring of export prices on third-market sales violated Article 11 of the Agreement.

The U.S. dumping provision died with the new 1991 agreement. When semiconductor demand picked up again, U.S. DRAM prices soared and proved so costly to purchasers that they ended the SIA's monopoly as the USTR's adviser on semiconductor trade policy. IBM, Tandem, and Hewlett-Packard led others in founding the Computer Systems Policy Project (CSPP) in 1989 to oppose the antidumping measures. The USTR could not possibly negotiate a satisfactory agreement in the face of sharply conflicting domestic interests. Rather than mediate, the USTR instructed the SIA and the CSPP to resolve their differences.

The SIA and the CSPP declared the antidumping provisions a "success." The CSPP was indifferent to the market access provisions so long as there were no sanctions for noncompliance. The 1991 accord extended by one year (to the end of 1992) the deadline for meeting the target, while stating that the target "constitute[s] neither a guarantee, a ceiling, nor a floor on the foreign market share."

Contrary to virtually all expectations, the foreign market share in Japan reached 20.2 percent in the fourth quarter of 1992. MITI pressure on other purchasers and a greater presence in Japan by U.S. firms probably accounted for the increase in U.S. market share. There is little evidence that the changing composition of Japanese demand (toward products the United States was better at producing, like microprocessors) did the trick.[19]

---

18. The employment effects of the agreement were probably negligible: back-of-the-envelope calculations suggest increased semiconductor employment of 2,300, but for each of these another was lost in computer manufacturing.

19. See Bergsten and Noland (1993, 136).

1.8   Conclusions

Those guilty of post hoc, ergo propter hoc reasoning attribute the rebound in the U.S. semiconductor industry since the mid-1980s to the agreement. The agreement did spawn greater cooperation and joint ventures between SIA and EIAJ members. But the U.S. industry did well to get out of memory chips (where the Japanese are now battling the South Koreans) and into microprocessors and application-specific integrated circuits. The agreement had little to do with this.

References

Bergsten, C. Fred, and Marcus Noland. 1993. *Reconcilable differences? United States-Japan economic conflict.* Washington, D.C.: Institute for International Economics.

Destler, I. M. 1992. *American trade politics.* 2nd ed. Washington, D.C.: Institute for International Economics.

Federal Interagency Staff Working Group. 1987. *The semiconductor industry.* Washington, D.C.: U.S. Government Printing Office, 16 November.

Hoshi, Takeo, Anil Kashyap, and David Scharfstein. 1990. The role of banks in reducing the costs of financial distress in Japan. *Journal of Financial Economics* 27 (September): 67–88.

Irwin, Douglas A. 1994. *Managed trade: The case against import targets.* Washington, D.C.: American Enterprise Institute.

Irwin, Douglas A., and Peter J. Klenow. 1994. Learning-by-doing spillovers in the semiconductor industry. *Journal of Political Economy* 102 (December): 1200–1227.

Ong, Paul M., and Don Mar. 1992. Post-layoff earnings among semiconductor workers. *Industrial and Labor Relations Review* 45 (January): 366–79.

Semiconductor Industry Association (SIA) and Dewey Ballantine. 1984. *Japanese market barriers in microelectronics. Memorandum in support of a petition pursuant to section 301 of the Trade Act of 1974, as amended, June 14, 1984.* Washington, D.C.: Semiconductory Industry Association and Dewey Ballantine.

Tyson, Laura D'Andrea. 1992. *Who's bashing whom?: Trade conflict in high-technology industries.* Washington, D.C.: Institute for International Economics.

2   The Rise and Fall of Big Steel's Influence on U.S. Trade Policy

Michael O. Moore

2.1   Introduction

The U.S. integrated carbon-steel sector has been one of the most common recipients of trade protection in America during the past twenty-five years. The industry's political strength has been demonstrated through the increasingly protectionist steel import regimes obtained in 1969, 1974, 1977, 1982, and 1984. These incidents are noteworthy in that each represents an import barrier outside of the normal U.S. import relief apparatus of escape clause and unfair trade petitions. They included, in particular, comprehensive voluntary export restraints and minimum import prices.

The main source of this political strength was the cohesive coalition of vertically-integrated carbon-steel producers, the steelworkers' union, and members of Congress from steel-producing regions. The cohesiveness of this "steel triangle" arose out of the technology and market structure of traditional integrated steel making. These factors included economies of scale of large-scale production, geographical concentration of plant sites, and the relative immobility of capital and labor employed in the traditional steel sector. They combined to create an industry of few firms, of workers possessing strong incentives to retain their jobs, and of politicians representing communities entirely dependent on steel.

Another factor that contributed to steel industry political effectiveness was the relative lack of cohesiveness among domestic interests opposing steel protection, in particular steel-using manufacturing industries. This highly diverse set of consumer industries has had little in common besides using steel as an input. Consequently, coalitions of steel users opposing protection have been ineffective, with one notable exception in 1989.

Michael O. Moore is associate professor of economics and international affairs at George Washington University.

The other critical aspect of the industry's success in procuring special protection was the very real possibility of obtaining tariffs through the U.S. antidumping and countervailing duty laws. Securing these duties has been a credible threat because of the widely acknowledged presence of massive foreign government steel subsidies, especially in Europe. The U.S. industry, therefore, could use the threat of legal import protection from such subsidies according to U.S. law. Since antidumping and countervailing duty orders are open-ended and extremely controversial abroad, successive U.S. presidential administrations were willing to head off their final imposition by negotiating special measures, especially voluntary import restraint agreements (VRAs).

Despite the series of successful attempts to obtain extraordinary import regimes, there is evidence that the U.S. integrated steel sector's ability to influence U.S. import may be waning. The outcome of the struggle to extend a steel VRA in 1989 is the first evidence of the diminished influence. The industry was forced to accept a much less restrictive import regime than that for which it had lobbied. The second piece of evidence occurred in 1993. Rather than lobby for and obtain a special import regime, the industry relied exclusively on administered protection (AP) procedures after the lapse of the VRA in 1992. This reliance suggests that the industry could not force the president to offer a special trade regime. In the end, this effort to obtain permanent antidumping and countervailing duties was of such limited success that the industry in 1994 faced the most liberal steel trade regime in over twenty-five years.

The loss of political clout is a consequence of changes in the factors that earlier had led to the sector's political cohesiveness. These changes include the rapidly evolving market structure in the United States, in particular the growing importance of a large number of nonintegrated steel producers known as "minimills." These firms have very different technological attributes and hence interests different from integrated firms. The growth of minimills has also resulted in a geographical dispersion of steel making in the United States which also lessens the political concentration of the industry. Second, the integrated sector's clout has been lessened too by the absolute drop in the number of steelworkers and hence the number of voters particularly interested in steel issues. Third, many years of intense import and domestic minimill competition has meant that the integrated producers have become much more efficient. This in turn undercuts the industry's call for special protection. Finally, the integrated sector increasingly has been confronted with an organized group of steel-using firms that provide a counterlobby to calls for special trade protection.

The aim of this paper is twofold. The first is to recount and explain the past success of the industry in obtaining special import regimes. The second is to consider how these factors have changed over the last fifteen years and how this change will likely affect the industry's clout in the future.

2.2   Steel Trade Policy: 1969 to 1984

The U.S. steel industry held a predominant position in the world in the early postwar period. Like many other manufacturing industries, the U.S. steel producers were the world's technological leaders as well as the largest producers and exporters. During this period, the industry generally supported trade liberalization as a means to open up export markets for U.S. steel products.

The U.S. steel industry's predominance began to wane during the 1950s as Europe and Japan became important producers. This new presence was a consequence both of a rebuilt industrial capacity as well as the result of an activist government industrial policy. The Japanese steel industry in particular was given extensive early government assistance to create an export industry, much of which would eventually find its way to the United States. Government sponsorship of the steel industry also occurred in some European countries, most notably in Italy, Great Britain, and France.[1]

U.S. producers' competitive position was also undercut by their having installed new "open-hearth" capacity in the 1940s, before the basic oxygen furnace, a major technological breakthrough, became widely available in the 1950s. Thus, new foreign capacity, especially in Japan, utilized a new technology that significantly reduced production costs.[2]

Nonetheless, the United States became a net importer of steel only in 1959 when a bitter 116-day steel strike caused U.S. steel users to turn to foreign sources for a stable steel supply. During the 1960s, high U.S. steel prices, continuing labor strife, aggressive foreign government support of its steel industries, and technological disadvantage led to a surge in imports from 7.3 percent of the U.S. market in 1964 to 16.7 percent in 1968 (AISI, various issues).

This growing import pressure led to what then was unprecedented cooperation between steel producers and the United Steelworkers (USW). Despite the history of intense and often violent labor-management strife, integrated producers and the USW joined forces to press for import restrictions during the late days of the Johnson administration. This effort was successful and in 1969 the executive branch negotiated the first of many voluntary restraint agreements with the European Community (EC) and Japan.

The VRAs, however, provided only limited import protection since they restricted only EC and Japanese imports and did not specify the product mix. Consequently, the VRA led both to an upgrading to higher value-added products by EC and Japanese exporters and to an increase in exports from noncovered exporters.

This quota regime lapsed in 1974 as high demand and high prices in other markets diverted steel imports from the United States.

---

1. See Howell et al. (1988) for details.
2. See Gold et al. (1984).

The next episode of protection occurred following the 1974 and 1975 recession. This recession was accompanied by a fundamental drop in the growth of world steel demand. Unfortunately, both U.S. and foreign producers interpreted the downturn in steel demand as part of a normal business cycle and continued to add new capacity.[3] When it became clear in the mid-1970s that the slowdown in steel demand growth was permanent, steel producers and governments all over the world were forced to cope with excess production capacity.

One consequence of world excess steel capacity was an increase in exports to the U.S. market. As table 2.1 shows, the volume of imports continued to grow in the United States through the mid-1970s even as U.S. steel consumption dropped.

U.S. producers and the USW argued that these increased imports were a result of the unfair practices of Japanese and European producers. In particular, charges were leveled that the steel imports were dumped into the United States at prices less than fair value. Both U.S. firms and the steelworkers' union argued that profits from the protected Japanese market allowed Japanese producers to lower prices in the United States and gain market share. The U.S. industry argued further that the massive subsidies by European nations with publicly owned steel firms (especially in France, the United Kingdom, and Italy) also resulted in unfairly priced imports. Both producers and the USW maintained that quantitative restrictions were necessary to prevent unfair imports into the United States.

Congressional allies of the integrated sector from steel-producing communities formed the Congressional Steel Caucus in the late 1970s to press the steel industry's case for strict import quotas. This caucus was bipartisan in nature and reflected the geographic concentration of the industry in the industrial heartland of traditional U.S. manufacturing.

The Carter administration, fearing that executive branch passivity might result in a congressionally mandated quota, urged the industry to file dumping cases under the revised antidumping rules in the Trade Act of 1974 (Crandall 1981). The industry followed this advice and filed a host of unfair trade cases in 1977. The Carter administration responded by fashioning a compromise which would avoid both quotas and final dumping duties. The compromise, known as the Trigger Price Mechanism (TPM), established a minimum import price based on a "trigger" price calculated from the production costs of the Japanese steel firms (then considered the world's low-cost suppliers). Any steel imports sold below this price would initiate an automatic antidumping investigation by the government. In return, the industry agreed to forego filing any new antidumping petitions.

Foreign producers were willing to cooperate in this system since, on the one hand, they would be better able to judge what was "acceptable" competition.

---

3. For example, Japanese gross steelmaking capacity expanded from 138 million metric tons in 1974 to 157 million tons in 1979, while European Community (EC) capacity increased from 178 million metrics to 203 million tons in 1979 (World Steel Dynamics 1994).

Table 2.1   U.S. Steel Industry in the Domestic Economy (millions of tons unless otherwise noted)

Year	Steel Imports	Import Market Share (%)	Total Steel Production	Apparent Final Steel Consumption	Steel Sector Employment (thousands)	Real Domestic Steel Sales (billions of 1982–84 $)	Steel/GDP[a]
1960	3.3	4.7	99.2	71.5	572	48.0	0.036
1964	6.4	7.3	127.1	87.9	555	52.9	0.038
1968	17.9	16.7	131.4	107.6	552	53.4	0.038
1974	13.4	15.9	145.7	119.6	512	77.5	0.037
1977	19.3	17.8	125.3	108.4	452	65.5	0.031
1981	18.9	19.8	120.8	105.4	391	47.4	0.027
1982	16.6	21.8	4.75	76.3	289	29.2	0.020
1984	26.2	26.4	92.5	98.9	236	28.9	0.024
1989	17.3	17.9	97.9	102.7	169	25.4	0.021
1990	17.1	17.5	98.9	97.5	164	23.4	0.020
1991	15.8	17.9	87.9	88.3	146	19.7	0.018
1992	17.1	18.0	92.9	95	140	18.9	0.018

Sources: American Iron and Steel Institute, Annual Statistical Report (various issues); Economic Report of the President (1993).

[a]Steel/GDP = million tons of steel consumption/billion $GDP (1987 prices).

Secondly, the TPM created a price floor based on low-cost producers which guaranteed high-cost European firms significant profits in the United States.

The system was attractive to the U.S. industry since it applied to *all* imports. Thus, the TPM discouraged trade diversion to other sources, unlike the 1969 VRA. However, upgrading by exporters to higher valued-added products was still possible and high cost producers could still "dump" their products as long as they charged above the trigger price.

Despite the respite from price competition created by the TPM, the integrated steel sector in the United States began in the 1980s with major competitive problems. In 1981, the U.S. steel sector continued to use decades-old open-hearth furnace technology in 36.5 percent of its operations, compared to 4.1 percent and 26.3 percent in Japan and the EC, respectively. Use of modern continuous casting techniques followed similar patterns: 20.3 percent in the United States versus 70.7 percent in Japan and 44.9 percent in the EC (International Iron and Steel Institute 1991). High labor costs were also an important problem for U.S. firms. Average unit labor costs for U.S. steel firms in 1979 were $162.7 per ton while Japanese rates averaged around $49.8 and Thyssen of Germany averaged $111.1 per ton (World Steel Dynamics 1990). Contributing factors to the high labor costs included outdated physical capital, rigid work rules, and wages that had risen under the Experimental Negotiating Agreement of 1974, which guaranteed a 3 percent nominal pay increase plus a full cost-of-living adjustment (regardless of productivity increases) in return for an agreement not to strike.

The U.S. industry was therefore ill equipped to cope with a major downturn and a renewal of intense international competition. The onset of the deep recession in 1981 and 1982 was nearly catastrophic for the U.S. industry. Operating profits for all steel firms fell to a loss of $3.38 *billion* in 1982 while total steel sector employment dropped sharply from 391,000 in 1981 to 289,000 in 1982, or nearly 25 percent. Import market share rose to 21.8 percent in 1982, thereby exceeding 20 percent of the U.S. market for the first time in history. This increased market share occurred despite the continued operation of the TPM. However, it is important to note that this overall increase in import share mainly reflected a precipitous drop in domestic consumption since the absolute level of all imports *fell* from 18.9 million tons to 16.6 million tons in the same period.

Despite the drop in import volume from all sources, the volume of European steel imports into the United States did increase substantially. This increased European production was in part possible because of the operation of the Davignon Plan in Europe, which prescribed internal European production quotas and allowed for some countries to provide operating subsidies to ease the adjustment costs of reduced employment. Much of the resulting surplus production was then exported, much of it to the United States.

The U.S. integrated industry therefore pointed to Europe, and especially the effects of government subsidies, as the main source of its difficulties. The combination of increased exports from the EC and massive losses in the U.S. steel industry induced U.S. producers to force the end of the TPM by filing sixty-one countervailing duty (CVD) and thirty-three antidumping (AD) duty petitions against eight countries of the EC, as well as Brazil and Romania.

The cases reached their first important juncture when the International Trade Commission (ITC) ruled affirmatively in twenty of the CVD cases and eighteen of the AD petitions at the preliminary stage. If final duties were implemented the result would have been potentially very chaotic for the EC since some nations would have been exempted from duties, and those that did receive punitive tariffs would be charged with widely varying rates based on the individual dumping and subsidy rulings of the Commerce Department. This divergent treatment for EC exports would have meant a closed U.S. market for a subset of European exporters, which, combined with a barrier-free intra-EC market, would have meant massive trade diversion within Europe.[4]

Had the Reagan administration allowed the AP process to continue to the final stage, it was very likely that open-ended and prohibitive duties on a subset of European steel exports would have been forthcoming. The Reagan administration also knew that many of the EC countries were providing subsidies to forestall possible major social unrest.

The Reagan administration, fearful of strained relations with the EC, agreed to enter negotiations with the EC for a new VRA. The agreement, finally reached in October 1982, limited EC exports to 5.5 percent of the U.S. market. In return, the U.S. firms dropped their unfair trade petitions and agreed to refrain from filing new cases against EC nations until the agreement expired in January 1986.

The agreement provided two important benefits to the U.S. industry. The VRA both allowed U.S. firms to avoid further AP litigation costs and provided protection against all EC imports rather than against only a subgroup, thereby avoiding some supply diversion. The VRA was also clearly preferable to the Europeans since it permitted them to continue to export and also prevented a major intra-European dispute.

The respite for the integrated industry was short-lived, however. As with the 1969 VRA, nonrestricted exports rapidly filled the void created by the fall in EC exports. Despite the VRA, imports from all sources rose slightly in 1983 to 17.1 million tons, although, with the recovering economy, the import market share actually fell to 20.5 percent.

Further complicating the industry's position was the start of the dollar's spectacular rise in value.

4. These diverse duties were in large part a reflection of the extremely dissimilar EC steel policies, with a subset of nations (Belgium, Italy, Great Britain, and France) providing substantial operating subsidies to their public owned steel firms while other nations with private steel firms (the Netherlands and Germany) were more laissez-faire in approach.

Integrated firms, severely disappointed by an import share still exceeding 20 percent, once again began to prepare trade cases. This time the USW and Bethlehem Steel filed an escape clause cause in which the ITC would rule on the presence of "serious" injury to the entire industry. If an affirmative ruling was forthcoming, President Reagan would be forced to rule on the case in September 1984, less than two months before the presidential election.

Simultaneously, Congressional Steel Caucus members prepared legislation imposing an across-the-board 15 percent quota on imported steel, an import share last seen in 1976. The congressional hearings for the bills were completely dominated by the steel sector and its supporters. Steel-using industries did provide some testimony in opposition but their lobbying efforts were extremely limited.

In July the ITC ruled that only five of the nine constituent steel "industries" were eligible for import relief. The ITC did find, however, that the industries producing pipe and tube, bar, rod, and rails were injured because of domestic competition, much of it from so-called minimills, rather than from import competition. Indeed, the ITC pointed out that minimills had consistently undersold both imports and integrated mills yet still remained profitable for the previous three years (ITC 1984, 47–54).

Rather than reject all import relief or impose barriers on only five steel sector categories as recommended by the ITC, the Reagan administration decided to negotiate a new global VRA. The plan, scheduled to expire in 1989, limited imports of finished steel to 18.4 percent of the domestic market. Even more important to the domestic industry was that the quota was on a *product-* and *country*-specific basis and that the agreement essentially covered all important steel exporting countries. Thus, the industry obtained a program that helped alleviate product upgrading and supply diversion, both of which had been major drawbacks of earlier VRAs and the TPM.

The 1984 VRA program was a major political victory for the integrated sector. Not only had the industry secured its most important long-term trade goal, namely, a comprehensive quota covering nearly all products and all exporting countries, but it also had wrested this outcome from Ronald Reagan, a distinctly market-oriented president.

2.3   Sources of Steel Industry Political Strength

The steel industry's ability to obtain increasingly protectionist import regimes arose from three factors. The first was the industry's political cohesiveness, which resulted from technological factors in the steel industry. The second was the legal import restrictions available to the industry. These options created a credible threat to use unfair trade remedy procedures to obtain discriminatory tariffs on import steel. Finally, the industry's sheer size resulted in important ballot box power.

2.3.1   Technology and Coalition Cohesion

Critical to the steel industry's success was the close cooperation of producers, workers, and politicians from steel-producing communities. These groups willingly worked together so closely largely because of the technology of integrated steel making. In particular, the large scale of an efficient steel mill, the geographical concentration of production, and the relative immobility of labor and capital within the industry all combined to provide strong incentives for all three groups to cooperate.

Integrated steel making involves transforming iron ore and coal into final products at one plant site. An integrated plant includes coke ovens, blast furnaces, basic-oxygen or open-hearth furnaces, a casting process, and rolling equipment. These technologies, especially coke ovens and blast furnaces, require a very large scale of operation. Thus an efficient integrated plant will employ thousands of workers and require enormous capital outlays. For example, the minimum efficient scale of a new integrated plant is about 7 million tons of capacity per year. An efficient new steel mill therefore represents about 7 percent of total U.S. annual steel consumption (Barnett and Crandall 1993).

The high costs of transporting iron and coal were a strong incentive to locate near these raw material sources; as a result, integrated steel operations are usually highly geographically concentrated. For example, in 1965 approximately 54 percent of U.S. steel capacity was located in Pennsylvania, Ohio, and Indiana (AISI 1969).[5]

The combination of large scale operations and geographical concentration had important consequences. High fixed costs meant a difficult entry into the integrated sector; the number of integrated firms therefore remained relatively low. Furthermore, large fixed costs translated into strong incentives for firms to maintain high capacity utilization rates. Firms would therefore often sell below average total costs in times of slow demand—the incentive for aggressive pricing behavior was ever present with integrated firms. These incentives created strong pressures for firms to act together to limit price competition through cartels and price setting. These two factors led to an oligopolistic market structure in the United States as well as in many other countries.

In terms of political lobbying, the small number of firms meant that there was little chance for a single integrated firm to get a free ride on lobbying efforts by other firms; shirking on lobbying efforts was easily detectable. Thus the American Iron and Steel Institute, the trade association of integrated steel makers, was composed of actors who knew each other well and could monitor contributions to lobbying efforts. The resulting cooperation was further enhanced by shared economic interests; integrated firms thus tended to speak with one voice on many public policy issues, including trade, environmental, and labor questions.

5. This pattern was repeated in the United States (e.g., Pittsburgh), in the United Kingdom (e.g., Manchester), and in continental Europe (e.g., Lorraine, Luxembourg, and the Ruhr valley).

The large scale of operations and geographical concentration also meant that integrated plants could easily dominate the economic life of a region, for example, Gary, Indiana, and Pittsburgh, Pennsylvania. Local political leaders were therefore very interested in cooperating with the integrated producers on lobbying efforts.

Workers in the industry also tended to have strong incentives to work for import protection. This arose out of two factors. First, the tendency for integrated works to dominate a region's economy meant that workers who lost their jobs in the steel mill might have few alternative employment opportunities. Second, since the advent of collective bargaining in the steel industry after World War II, the USW has managed to secure relatively high wages, nearly double the average manufacturing wage. These high wages were particularly attractive since many steel industry jobs have traditionally been relatively unskilled though often quite dangerous. Since the industry was organized almost exclusively by the USW, labor also had an effective single voice to contribute to policy debates.

The relative stability of the actors—the same producers, the same union, the same congressional districts—meant that those involved in lobbying for steel sector protection were well-known to each other. This helped create reputations for cooperation and enhanced coalition solidarity. The single voice and shared interests also meant that the steel sector could share lobbying costs either explicitly through joint press conferences, for example, or implicitly through canvassing congressional members or executive branch officials.

The relative influence of the united steel coalition was further enhanced by the highly varied nature of the steel user. These industries, whose only shared interest is the use of steel as an input, generally found it very difficult to cooperate on steel import policy. All of the advantages of the steel sector (common economic interests, small number of firms, and stable actors) have traditionally been entirely absent among steel users.

Probably the most striking examples of the cooperation among the producers, the steelworkers' union, and political representatives can be found in congressional hearings about steel import policy. Testimony before Congress in 1984 for the 15 percent quota bill, for example, showed the near complete solidarity of steel producers, the United Steelworkers, and local politicians. Indeed, the only major controversy among steel interests in 1984 was whether firms should be forced to reinvest profits from their steel operations back into worker retraining and modernization efforts. (The USW strongly supported both of these requirements while the industry generally was fiercely opposed.)

2.3.2   Trade Remedy Law Advantages

Another critical aspect of the U.S. industry's success at obtaining protection has been its credible threat of obtaining antidumping or countervailing duties on imported steel. This credibility arises out of technical legal aspects of the unfair trade remedy laws as well as out of the widely acknowledged level of government steel sector intervention in many countries.

Technical aspects of the unfair trade laws that worked to the steel industry's advantage are numerous. Indeed, in the United States the steel industry has by far been the most frequent petitioner in antidumping and countervailing duty petitions.

The first advantage for the steel industry is that the cases are adjudicated on a product- and country-specific basis. This means that each country and each firm may receive widely varying duties. This translates into the possibility that some firms and countries can be completely frozen out of the U.S. market while others can freely come in.

This was particularly important for the steel industry, wherein a myriad of products are imported from many countries. The industry could then argue that because the administered protection procedures would lead to chaos in the industry, comprehensive special import regimes should be used instead.

The unfair trade procedures were also attractive to the steel industry as a means of forcing the president to negotiate special trade agreements. The reason is that the unfair trade remedies are quasi-judicial, bureaucratic, and rules-oriented. In particular, the ITC rules on the presence of "material" injury at a preliminary and final stage while the Commerce Department rules on the existence and size of dumping or subsidy margins. If both agencies rule affirmatively on the petition, duties are assessed on imports that are firm- and country-specific. These duties have no set time limit. Consequently, the president has no role to play whatsoever in the formal adjudication of these petitions so that foreign policy or national security concerns are totally absent from the decision process.

The combination of these factors has meant that a number of different presidents have faced the possibility of widely varying and high duties placed on important U.S. allies. Since these duties are potentially prohibitively high and open-ended, the political price for allowing them to be imposed has encouraged administrations to negotiate quotas before the duties become final dumping and countervailing duty orders.

The use of antidumping and countervailing duty petitions would not be important, however, without foreign practices which can make positive dumping and subsidy margins very likely. On the one hand, subsidy margins are highly likely since many nations have subsidized their steel industries—in Europe, as a means of slowing employment losses, and in the developing world as a means of industrial policy.

Positive dumping margins are also highly probable because of the incentives (explained in section 2.3.1) to price below average total costs in times of recession. In addition, since the Commerce Department uses "fully-allocated-costs," that is, average total costs, in its production costs calculation, the legal rules for calculating dumping margins will work toward positive dumping margins, especially if recessions occur concurrently across the world.

2.3.3   Ballot Box Strength

The political power of the industry has also been enhanced by the sheer number of potential voters in the industry. In 1974, for example, there were over half a million Americans directly employed in the steel industry. In addition, the concentration of these workers in relatively localized geographical regions meant that steel interests were particularly important in elections for the House of Representatives. Thus the industry has been able to marshal the political support of a major part of the congressional delegations of West Virginia, Pennsylvania, Ohio, and Indiana. These congressional members have a common interest in steel import policy and have been able to pressure the entire Congress to help the steel industry. The large number of workers in each of these states also meant that senatorial candidates and senators had strong incentives to support the industry.

The concentration of these workers in populous states with many electoral votes (e.g., Pennsylvania, Ohio, and Indiana) has translated into importance in presidential politics as well. The most notable example is the 1984 filing of an escape clause petition that forced President Reagan to confront steel import policy just weeks before the election.

2.4   The 1989 VRA Renewal Campaign

The VRA program announced in 1984 was set to lapse in 1989. This, the Reagan administration had hoped, would prevent the steel industry from bringing pressure to bear on the next presidential campaign. However, in the late summer and early fall of 1988, Republican presidential candidate George Bush was significantly behind Michael Dukakis in the polls. Governor Dukakis had already pledged support to a renewal of the VRA.

As part of the general effort to coordinate a come-from-behind victory and to help solidify political support among "Reagan Democrats" in the steel region, the Bush campaign agreed to support a VRA extension but did not outline any specifics about the timing and details of the proposed program.

Soon after the inauguration, posturing began over the extension's exact details. The usual array of actors lined up in favor of the VRA extension. The bipartisan Congressional Steel Caucus, the integrated firms' trade association (AISI), and the steelworkers' union reassembled the coalition that had been so successful five years earlier. The main goals of the steel industry and its allies were to push for a five-year extension of the existing program, with the inclusion of nonparticipating nations (Canada and Sweden) into the extended VRA.

However, unlike earlier steel import policy debates, steel users for the first time were well organized to counter the steel industry's position. In particular, the Coalition of American Steel-Using Manufacturers (CASUM), headed by Caterpillar Inc., argued that the president should terminate the VRA program because (1) steel-using firms provided much more employment than steel-producing firms and the VRAs hurt U.S. exports; (2) the steel quotas had increased prices and led to spot shortages, especially for firms using modern inventory management techniques ("just-in-time" delivery); (3) the steel industry should rely, like virtually all other domestic industries, on the established administered protection procedures to address their trade complaints; and (4) the high steel sector profits in 1988 and improving domestic steel industry competitiveness were evidence that the domestic industry did not deserve special help.

The overall strategy of CASUM was to turn the debate away from the actions of foreign firms and governments toward the VRAs' effects on United States manufacturing interests. CASUM also appealed indirectly to protectionist elements in Congress by emphasizing that VRAs rewarded unfair traders through the transfer of profits earned in the protected U.S. market. The coalition also made a concerted effort to identify steel-using firms in the districts of Congress members who had supported the steel industry in the past. This helped provide constituent counterbalance to the votes of the steel-producing industry.

In the final analysis, the VRA was continued as candidate George Bush had promised, but it was a far cry from the program backed by the industry. In particular, the new program granted a two-and-a-half-year extension (rather than five years), loosened the market share of the quota by a 1 percent *increase* per year (instead of tightening the quantitative restrictions), and liberalized the short-supply provisions (rather than maintaining the status quo). In short, the 1989 VRA extension was a major disappointment for the integrated industry and a major victory for the steel-using industries.

The actual experience of the VRA in the post-1989 period strongly suggests that not only was the program less than what the integrated firms wanted, but that the quotas may have had very little effect on the domestic steel market. In particular, the quotas were not filled on a country or product basis for most of the post-1987 period.

The quotas were binding or nearly binding for most of the first two years. However, beginning in 1988, the overall quota fill rate fell from 79 percent to a low of 54 percent in the last three months of the VRA in 1992. In addition, subsequent to the extension in October 1989, no country filled its overall quota and in only one instance (Finland in the October–December 1990 period) did imports reach over 90 percent of the quota limits. This pattern is repeated for individual product categories. After 1988, the quotas were binding or near binding only in some speciality products—alloy tool steel, tin plate, and stainless steel plate and sheet.[6]

The other major aspect of the Bush administration's steel policy was the multilateral steel negotiations conducted parallel to the VRA program. The Bush administration hoped that a Multilateral Steel Agreement (MSA) would eliminate the underlying problems that had bedeviled steel trade for twenty

6. For a detailed list, see Moore (1996).

years, especially global overcapacity, tariff and nontariff barriers, and trade-distorting practices such as dumping and subsidies. The entire industry strongly supported this effort. Indeed, a multilateral solution to steel problems had long been the principal long-term public policy goal of all members of the domestic steel industry, including the USW, the integrated producers, and minimills.

As the April 1992 demise of the VRA program approached, the Bush administration held fast to the position that all quantitative restrictions *permanently* end on April 1. Surprisingly little support emerged in the steel industry for another extension of the VRA program. Only the United Steelworkers, Bethlehem Steel, and the specialty steel sector publicly supported an extension of the quotas. The balance of the integrated industry, extremely disappointed in its experience with the VRA after 1988, expressed no interest whatsoever in an extension.[7] Instead, the steel firms announced repeatedly that they would file another round of antidumping and countervailing duty petitions, but this time they vowed to pursue them to final decisions. In other words, the industry threatened that it would try to obtain the definitive AD and CVD duties that would provide significant and lasting protection.

In the event, the VRA program expired on April 1, 1992, and the multilateral steel negotiations ended with no agreement. As promised, the Bush administration refused to take special action and, also as promised, the steel industry filed over eighty antidumping and countervailing duty petitions in the summer of 1992.

The superficial parallels to 1984 are striking. Once again a free-trade-oriented Republican president faced reelection while a torrent of steel industry AP petitions wound through the bureaucracy. Further complicating the political calculus was that Bush faced both a weak economy and a much more formidable opponent in Clinton than Reagan had faced with Mondale in 1984. Indeed, many veteran industry observers fully expected that the administration would be forced to reach an accommodation with the steel industry before the AP process worked to a conclusion.[8] The implicit assumption, of course, was that high final antidumping duties were near certain and that the administration would be unwilling to allow them to be imposed. These expectations for a negotiated outcome grew even stronger as the polls continued to show President Bush lagging behind Governor Clinton.

If the steel industry wanted to use the AP petitions to inject steel policy into the 1992 presidential campaign, they failed utterly. President Bush held firm to his pledge not to extend any special deals to the industry.

---

7. The integrated firms' *private* position insistence is somewhat in dispute. Steel producer representatives argue that the firms had no interest in an extension. However, an official at the Trade Representative's office insists that the industry was in favor of extension until December 1991, when it became clear that the Bush administration would not grant it.

8. For example, see the comments of long-time steel editor George McManus in *Iron Age*, May 1992.

With the election of Bill Clinton, a politically powerful integrated steel industry might have used the opportunity to force steel import policy into policy avenues with political discretion and away from the administered protection process. Instead, the industry pressed ahead with the AP petitions.

The cases proceeded to the ITC for a final ruling on material injury. On July 27, 1993, the ITC ruled affirmatively on thirty-two cases and negatively on forty-one petitions, which translated into roughly half of the imports in value terms. The majority of the ITC's members concluded that dumped and subsidized imports were not important causes of domestic problems in the industry. Instead, the majority of the ITC reasoned that price competition among domestic firms was the main source of difficulty and pointed out that imports were sold at prices that were often *higher* than domestic sources (ITC 1993). In other words, the ITC found strong evidence that the domestic steel industry was increasingly prone to intense *domestic* price competition—the fragmented nature of the "new" U.S. steel market made oligopolistic price discipline very difficult to maintain.

In sum, the spotty protection (final high duties placed on some countries' products and all provisional duties removed on others) meant that the integrated industry could count on very little significant comprehensive protection from these cases. The duties' lasting effect will depend in large part on whether countries not covered by final duties will step in to replace the displaced imports. If they do so, the domestic price effects of the duties may be minimal.

For the first time in about twenty-five years steel had clearly and publicly lost a major trade policy debate. The industry's most important trump card, the threat of final and near-prohibitive dumping and countervailing duties, had been played and little had come of it. While the industry was able to raise prices and garner significant short-term increases in profits during the period of provisional duties, the strategy did not lead to permanent *comprehensive* protection.

2.5   The Changing Nature of Integrated Steel Sector Influence

The integrated steel industry clearly was not as successful in influencing trade policy in the post-1989 period. The reasons for that diminished influence are directly related to changes in the industry's sources of strengths, mentioned in section 2.3 above.

2.5.1   Technological Evolution in the Carbon Steel Industry

The most important changes are without question in the evolving technology and market structure of the carbon steel sector. In particular, the spectacular rise in the minimill sector and the increasing importance of "reconstituted" mills have seriously undercut the cohesion of the traditional steel-industry lobbying coalition.

Minimills do not produce raw steel but instead melt steel scrap using high-temperature electric arc furnaces (EAFs). The molten steel is then cast and rolled to produce final steel products in a fashion similar to an integrated mill. However, unlike many older integrated mills, the minimills' recent emergence means that they use continuous casting techniques almost exclusively.[9] Because minimills do not use coke ovens or blast furnaces, the minimum efficient scale for an EAF is around 1 million tons were year instead of 7 million for an integrated plant. Since minimills are not dependent on iron ore and coal, they can establish plants near the end market. Minimills also typically have more flexible work rules and incentive-based pay, which reduces unit labor costs for both their nonunion and union work forces.

So-called reconstituted mills also have played a much more prominent role in the steel sector. These firms arose as the integrated companies sold individual plants to reduce costs and as some established firms declared bankruptcy. The resulting firms, including Weirton Steel and Gulf States Steel, have become increasingly competitive with the established integrated firms.

The success of the minimills in the U.S. market has been remarkable. Minimill shipments rose from 7 percent of the U.S. domestic market in 1979 to 24 percent by 1991. Reconstituted mills, essentially nonexistent in 1979, controlled 25 percent of the domestic market in 1991.[10]

The most important consequence of this more fragmented steel sector is that the traditional cohesion of the industry has largely been dissipated. This has manifested in a number of ways. First, the large number of firms makes price discipline so much more difficult that the oligopolistic power of the integrated firms has largely disappeared. The dramatic drop in entry and exit costs means that the U.S. steel sector is much more similar to the textbook example of a competitive market. Second, the rising importance of minimills means that steel production is much less geographically concentrated. Third, the radically different market structures of the new entrants mean that the industry's members do not necessarily share the same positions on steel policy issues.[11] The most important example of such dissension is that of Ken Iverson, CEO of Nucor Steel. Iverson is an impassioned free trader and has often spoken out against steel protection.[12] Finally, the success of the minimills vis-à-vis both

---

9. For a comparison of minimill and integrated mill production techniques, see Hogan (1987).

10. Moore (1996).

11. One recent example concerns the health care reform effort in 1994. Many integrated firms, with large numbers of retired workers, were outspoken in their support of the "employer mandate" requiring all firms to contribute to health care. Minimill firms, with a younger workforce and less generous benefits, were much more reluctant to support such changes. Other examples of differences involve environmental and energy policy. Minimills are not affected by the air pollution control costs of coke ovens, and integrated mills are less sensitive to electricity price reform.

12. Mr. Iverson spoke out strongly against any trade protection during congressional hearings in 1984 and asserted that "we believe that tariff or nontariff trade barriers will delay modernization of our steel industry, [and] will cost the consumer billions of dollars." Instead, he argued that the government could offer assistance in retraining programs and various special tax credits directed specifically at the integrated sector (House Ways and Means 1984, 288–89).

integrated domestic mills and imports has undercut the argument of the integrated sector to point to imports as the source of any economic difficulties.

2.5.2   Changing Voting Strength

As the industry has changed over the last fifteen years, the voting strength of the industry has diminished.

The most obvious change is the absolute drop in the number of steel sector employees. Total steel sector employment has fallen from 572,000 in 1960 to 236,000 in 1984, and in 1992 was only 140,000. In addition, these employment drops have been concentrated in the northeast, where electoral votes have dropped concurrently as the population has migrated to the southern and western United States. These two factors together mean that steel industry concerns are much less important in presidential campaigns.

The changing local character of steel sector production has been important at the congressional level as well. As many of the integrated mills have been closed, fewer and fewer congressional districts have a large number of steelworkers dominating the economic life of a region. This translates into fewer members of Congress who will likely fight aggressively for import restraints. The concurrent rise in minimills has meant that more and more smaller steel firms are geographically dispersed. This may mean that more congressional districts have an active steel industry presence, but the political importance of a three-hundred-worker minimill and a two-thousand-worker integrated works are hardly comparable. In addition, the small entry and exit costs of a minimill mean that if a firm closes it is much more likely to resume operation than if a large integrated plant is idled.

2.5.3   Trade Remedy Laws: The Future of Steel Protection

Integrated firms may become even more aggressive in pursuing antidumping and countervailing duty orders than in the past, especially if foreign governments continue to artificially support their industries, making a successful AD or CVD petition likely.

However, if the integrated industry pursues these petitions to final decisions, as in 1993, this will be a sign of political weakness, not of strength. The nature of the trade remedy laws means that even politically weak industries have full legal access to the process. Pursuit of final unfair trade duties thus will mean that integrated firms will be relying on the quasi-judicial and nonpolitical part of the U.S. trade policy apparatus rather than using their clout to obtain special import regimes.

The industry also may devote considerable resources to changing the technical details of unfair trade remedies. Examples in the 1990s have included lobbying for retaining the principle of "cumulation" in material injury decisions, changing the rules on captive imports, and continuing to press for an outright ban on all subsidies to foreign steel firms.

Even if the integrated firms are more successful in the future at obtaining unfair trade remedies, they still will face intense competition from domestic minimills. This is likely to be true even in flat-rolled products, long a source of competitive strength for the integrated mills. Indeed, technological changes over the last five years in thin-slab casting and scrap-replacement iron sources will make minimills increasingly important in the high value-added sector as well.

2.6   Conclusion

The U.S. integrated steel sector has long been one of the most important and successful proponents of import protection. The industry's success at obtaining special import quotas has been rivaled only by the textile and apparel industry.

Despite past successes, fundamental and profound changes in the technology and market structure of the industry point to a diminished steel sector political influence. Most important, the spectacular growth of minimills has created a much more fragmented steel industry. The industry has become and will likely continue to be less geographically concentrated, with fewer workers and more firms. All of these factors work to create more competition within the domestic market. This in turn makes effective coalition building more complicated and lobbying efforts less cohesive. In short, the days of the integrated firms' ability to wrest special import regimes from reluctant presidents may be over.

Ironically, the weakened political strength of the industry has been accompanied by a substantial improvement in the international competitiveness of the U.S. steel industry. Not only have minimills arisen as efficient producers of many steel products, but integrated firms themselves have undertaken substantial modernization and restructuring efforts. Labor as well has done its part by agreeing to a number of painful concessions to improve productivity. Finally, the industry has been further helped by the lower value of the dollar during the late 1980s and early 1990s.

Though the era of comprehensive steel import quotas may be over, a politically weakened, but still politically significant, industry will continue to press its case for protection. Unlike earlier efforts, the industry will likely pursue antidumping and countervailing duty petitions to final conclusions rather than using them as political leverage for quotas.

In short, the decade of the 1980s was pivotal for the U.S. steel industry. The industry began the decade as a barely functioning oligopoly, at the height of its political, if not economic, influence. The restructuring of the decade has yielded a much more competitive industry. This reborn industry, stripped of much of its oligopolistic price discipline and political cohesion, in the future will rely on the normal trade remedy apparatus.

Chronology of Steel Trade Events

1969	Negotiation of VRAs with the EC and Japan (scheduled to last until 1974)
1977	Inauguration of Trigger Price Mechanism for all steel imports
January 1982	Dozens of antidumping and countervailing duty petitions filed against EC countries
October 1982	Negotiation of VRA with the EC (scheduled to last through December 1985)
January 1984	Escape clause petition filed by Bethlehem Steel and United Steelworkers
July 1984	ITC rules affirmatively in the escape clause petition in five out of nine product categories (affirmative: sheet and strip, plate, structural shapes, wire and wire products, and semi-finished steel; negative: pipe and tube, bar, rod, and rails)
September 1984	Negotiation of VRAs on all nine steel products in escape clause petition; market share for participating nations 18.4 percent (set to end in September 1989)
November 1988	Candidate Bush promises to continue VRA
July 1989	President Bush announces Steel Liberalization Program: (*a*) 2.5 year VRA extension, (*b*) 1 percent annual increase for countries willing to stop unfair practices (up to 20.9 percent by March 1992), (*c*) Multilateral Steel Negotiations (MSA) begun to remove "trade-distorting" steel practices
April 1992	Termination of VRA; breakdown of MSA over allowable ("green light") subsidies
June 1992	Antidumping and countervailing petitions filed against flat-rolled products
July 1993	ITC rules affirmatively on only a subset of steel industry petitions

References

American Iron and Steel Institute (AISI). *Annual statistical report.* Various years. Washington, D.C.: American Iron and Steel Institute.

Barnett, Donald F., and Robert W. Crandall. 1986. *Up from the ashes: The rise of the steel minimill in the United States.* Washington, D.C.: Brookings Institution.

———. 1993. Steel: Decline and renewal. In *Industry studies,* ed. Larry L. Duetsch. Englewood Cliffs, N.J.: Prentice Hall.

Crandall, Robert W. 1981. *The U.S. steel industry in recurrent crises: Policy options in a competitive world.* Washington, D.C.: Brookings Institution.

Gold, Bela, William Pierce, Gerhard Rosegger, and Mark Perlman. 1984. *Technological progress and industrial leadership: The growth of the U.S. steel industry 1900–1970.* Lexington, Mass.: D.C. Heath.

Hogan, William T. 1987. *Minimills and integrated mills: A comparison of steel making in the United States.* Lexington, Mass.: Lexington Books.

House Ways and Means Committee. 1984. *Problems of the U.S. Steel Industry.* Serial 98-93.

Howell, Thomas R., William A. Noeller, and Alan Wm. Wolfe. 1988. *Steel and the state: Government intervention and steel's structural crisis.* Boulder, Colo.: Westview Press.

International Iron and Steel Institute. 1991. *Steel statistical yearbook.* Brussels: International Iron and Steel Institute.

Moore, Michael O. 1996. Steel protection in the 1980s: The waning influence of big steel? NBER Working Paper no. 4760. In *The political economy of American trade policy,* ed. Anne O. Krueger. Chicago: University of Chicago Press, forthcoming.

Tsoukalis, Loukas, and Robert Strauss. 1985. Crisis and adjustment in European steel: Beyond laisser faire. *Journal of Common Market Studies* 23, no. 3:207–28.

U.S. International Trade Commission (ITC). 1984. *Carbon and certain alloy steel products.* USITC Publication no. 15513. Washington, D.C.: U.S. Government Printing Office.

———. 1993. *Certain flat-rolled carbon steel products from Argentina, Australia, Austria, Belgium, Brazil, Canada, Finland, France, Germany, Italy, Mexico, Netherlands, New Zealand, Poland, Romania, Spain, Sweden, and the United Kingdom.* ITC Publication no. 2664. Washington, D.C.: U.S. Government Printing Office.

World Steel Dynamics. 1990. *Core report NN.* New York: Paine-Webber.

———. 1992. *Battle of the minis.* New York: Paine-Webber.

———. 1994. *Core report VV.* New York: Paine-Webber.

3 Making Sense of the 1981 Automobile VER: Economics, Politics, and the Political Economy of Protection

Douglas R. Nelson

The U.S. automobile industry is highly concentrated (three firms account for the great bulk of automobile manufacturing in the United States), employs a large number of people (over 300,000 in 1978), and has major production facilities in many states (major assembly plants in twelve states and suppliers in virtually every state). The work force is highly organized and represented by a politically active union (the United Auto Workers [UAW]), and each of the majors maintains an individual lobbying presence in Washington as well as a collective presence via the Motor Vehicle Manufacturers' Association (MVMA). When one adds the intangible effect of the strong attachment Americans have to the automobile and the perception of its place in modern American economic development, it is clear that this industry meets virtually everyone's conditions for effective political power. In the late 1970s, faced with slumping sales and profits, rising labor costs, and increased import competition, the industry actively pursued, and ultimately received, protection from Japanese import competition in the form of a voluntary export restraint (VER). At this level of detail, the story seems to be easily rationalized by the simplest form of short-run, profit-seeking political economy (e.g., Chicago school or instrumentalist Marxist). A more detailed study, however, suggests that the reality is considerably more complex.

Simple political-economy models assume that

1. agents (e.g., firms, factor owners, consumers) are rational in the sense that they know how the world works and pursue their self-interests by allocating resources between economic and political activities so as to maximize their wealth;[1]

Douglas R. Nelson is associate professor of economics at Tulane University.

1. More sophisticated theoretical models emphasize maximization of *welfare*. However, since this is not a particularly operational concept, we follow the general strategy of emphasizing wealth as the goal of economic and political-economic activity.

2. the political-economic environment is simple and transparent, in particular, that
   a. the economic environment is simple, nonstochastic, and understood by all participants and analysts,
   b. "Money talks" is a satisfactory general model of the political process, which is generally taken to be nonstochastic,
   c. political structure, both with respect to particular decisions and the general environment of the decision, is of second-order analytical importance compared with the balance of political pressure.
3. points 1 and 2 imply a simple methodological rule: economic outcomes are informative with respect to the political intentions of agents. Thus, identify the gainers and assert that their political action caused the policy.[2]

Point 1 seems unproblematic, and probably unavoidable in any systematic study of political or economic action. However, it is hard to make the politics of the auto VER fit easily within the analytical confines of point 2, with the implication that the methodological program following point 2 is seriously undermined. This paper briefly argues that the automobile industry (or at least most of it) successfully pursued a protectionist trade policy agenda, and that the immediate economic return on that agenda was small and known to be small, but that the political (and longer-run economic) return was potentially large, though risky. Furthermore, we will conclude by arguing that the industry failed in this larger political strategy.

3.1   Getting Protection

The exceptionally powerful position of the U.S. automobile industry in the U.S. political-economic structure does not imply that the industry can achieve any conceivable goal, or even that it can achieve a very modest goal with certainty. In addition to the (usually weak) direct resistance from those interests directly harmed by government intervention on behalf of a particular industry, political structure, political norms, and, at least in the case of trade policy, the international commitments of the executive branch all put constraints on particularistic outcomes.[3] In addition, the complex relationships between issues and between branches (and subbranches) of government render certainty with respect to significant outcomes virtually impossible. As a result, the political strategies, even of the very powerful, reflect these constraints in both the choice of goals to pursue and in the allocation of resources across venues and over time. Both the power of the auto industry and the constraints imposed by

---

2. Stigler (1975) suggests that we "look, as precisely and carefully as we can, at who gains and who loses, and how much, when we seek to explain a regulatory policy" so that "the truly intended effects can be deduced from the actual effects."

3. This is, of course, why particularistic interests generally invest considerable effort in the attempt to dress up the plain fact of greed in the fancy language of national interest.

political and economic structures are well illustrated in the case of the 1981 automobile VER with Japan.

We begin with the institutional constraints. The first step in most protection seeking involves some form of administered protection, the most common form of which is one of the Title 7 mechanisms (i.e., antidumping and countervailing duty procedures). However, politically powerful industries often pursue a strategy in which the administered protection process is only the first step in a more involved political process. In these cases, the administrative mechanism of choice is often the escape clause mechanism and in the auto case Ford and the UAW filed an escape clause suit with the International Trade Commission (ITC) in June 1980.[4] In addition to whatever direct pressure the industry might bring to bear on the executive, an essential part of the high-track political strategy is mobilization of congressional support. Thus, even before filing the escape clause suit, the industry actively promoted congressional hearings on auto industry trade, which the Subcommittee on Trade of the House Committee on Ways and Means commenced in March 1980. In fact, the ITC, on a three-to-two vote, determined that foreign vehicles were "not being imported into the United States in such increased quantities as to be a substantial cause of serious injury, or the threat thereof, to the domestic industries producing articles like or directly competitive with the imported articles" (USITC 1980).

While surprising to many, the ITC's negative injury determination was not the end of protection seeking on the political track, rather the emphasis shifted to an even greater focus on the executive via direct lobbying, and indirect pressure through public opinion and Congress. The very visible and public difficulties of the auto industry combined with a growing bilateral trade deficit in U.S.-Japan trade created fertile ground for public claims of unfair trading practices in autos. Trade policy was beginning to emerge as an attractive issue for political entrepreneurs after a hiatus of half a century, and two of the first entrepreneurs to recognize its potential were Senators John Danforth and Lloyd Bentsen, who introduced legislation to quantitatively restrict auto imports in February 1981. Probably the most significant political change in the period following the filing, and ultimate failure, of the escape clause petition was Ronald Reagan's defeat of Jimmy Carter in the 1980 presidential election. Unlike the Carter administration, the new Reagan administration lacked a strong commitment to trade liberalization as an issue and proved to be considerably more willing to consider trade protection as a policy response to an industry's

4. This refers to Section 201 of the Trade Act of 1974, which permits the U.S. government, under Article 19 of the General Agreement on Tariffs and Trade (GATT), to provide protection to producers that are "seriously injured" or "threatened with serious injury" by increased imports. If the U.S. International Trade Commission (ITC) determines that such injury has occurred, it recommends an action to the president, who then must decide whether to accept the ITC's recommendation, take some other action, or do nothing. Finger, Hall, and Nelson (1982) argue that the escape clause mechanism has functioned as part of a political track to protection, while the Title 7 mechanisms constitute a technical track. Nelson (1989) presents a detailed analysis of the political track for the case of the auto industry.

problems than had the Carter administration.[5] Faced with both domestic (e.g., tax reform) and international (e.g., anticommunism and national security) issues that it considered more pressing, the Reagan administration chose to cede dominance on the trade issue to Congress. Thus the Reagan administration chose to respond to industry and congressional pressure on the auto issue by negotiating a voluntary export restraint with Japan.

Interestingly, the administration's rhetorical commitment to free markets did produce some difficulties in its negotiations with Japan over the VER. Specifically, the administration refused to be seen as publicly demanding such restriction and, in particular, as naming a particular level of restraint. Ultimately, however, following a "nonauto-related" trip to Japan by U.S. Trade Representative Brock in March 1981, the Japanese government announced that it would voluntarily restrict exports of automobiles to the United States to 1.68 million units (a reduction of 7.7 percent on the previous period) for the first year of a three-year agreement, with some unspecified growth in the next two years. In the event, given the continued poor performance of the U.S. industry, the Japanese government retained the limit through all three years.

The story to this point is fully consistent with the simple political-economy model sketched in the introduction: a well-organized, politically powerful industry identified a politically feasible goal, pursued it effectively, and was successful. So far, so good. Unfortunately, when we look at the payoff, the litmus test for the Chicago school model, the account begins to break down.

3.2   The Economic Effects of Automobile Protection

The standard approach to evaluating the welfare effects of the VER involves a straightforward extension of the textbook partial equilibrium analysis of triangles and rectangles. The basic strategy takes observed price and quantity data as equilibrium values and explicit assumptions on functional forms and estimates of elasticities of demand and supply. Under a variety of assumptions on elasticities and cross-elasticities, as well as the initial state of demand, these studies yield estimates of consumer costs from $1 to nearly $6 billion, consumer costs per job saved ranging from $95,000 to $220,000, and increases in domestic profit and rent transfers to Japanese firms both on the order of $2 billion.[6] As a result of the continuing recession, the estimates for the years immediately following the imposition of the VRA are consistently lower than those for later years.

The research that generates such estimates is essentially static in nature; it

5. Trade proves to be an interesting litmus test of an administration's orientation, whether *promarket* or *probusiness*. Where the Carter administration showed a strong promarket orientation in trade as well as regulation, at least on trade the Reagan administration was clearly more probusiness.

6. See Case M-22 (Automobiles) in Hufbauer, Berliner, and Elliott (1986) for a convenient survey of the input data that have appeared in the literature.

does not address the more difficult question of the effect of protection on the long-term competitiveness of the U.S. auto industry. One of the problems in carrying out such an analysis is, of course, determining the time horizon over which to make the relevant evaluations. For example, even the static direct effects of protection vary fairly considerably over time, primarily as a function of general macroeconomic conditions. We can, however, informally consider trends in three essential correlates of competitiveness: wages and labor productivity, investment, and quality. With respect to wages, the industry experienced a short term gain in the immediate aftermath of the VER by extracting substantial wage concessions from the UAW. With the protection in place, and the recovery of profits following the improvement in general macroeconomic conditions, the UAW was able to negotiate quite generous wage increases in the 1984 agreements with Ford and General Motors. Given our previous conclusion that the jump in profits primarily reflects increased rent extraction from U.S. consumers, this suggests that the postwar pattern of rent sharing between labor and capital in the auto industry continued more or less unchanged. Thus it would be difficult to conclude that the industry gained much in terms of its relations with labor from either import competition or the subsequent protection.

To a considerable extent the senescent industry argument for protection relies on the protected industry using the period of protection to make fundamental adjustments in the organization of production to improve its competitiveness. It is certainly the case that all three U.S. majors have attempted to make both physical and organizational changes in response to competition from Japanese firms. The industry did undertake considerable new capital spending in the immediate post-VER period and again in the early 1990s and it is likely that these changes have improved its competitiveness, though some of the investment in robots and other new technologies has proven disappointing. The final dimension related to long-run competitiveness is quality, and the perception thereof. At least as important as the industry's product-mix problems were the deterioration in quality and the widespread perception of the U.S. majors as suppliers of high-priced, low-quality automobiles. Here the record is mixed. By the 1990s the perception of quality seems to have improved. However, an analysis of *Consumer Reports* data on frequency of repair suggests considerable improvement in quality by Chrysler in the late 1980s and early 1990s, while Ford and GM show no clear trend. While there has been some deterioration of overall Japanese quality, the most striking fact revealed by this analysis is the continuing gap in quality between U.S. and Japanese producers of automobiles.

Overall, there is no question but that the VER resulted in a substantial increase in industry profits once the U.S. economy recovered from recession and auto demand increased. However, it would also appear to be clear that those profits primarily reflect increased rent extraction from U.S. consumers. Most important, Ford and possibly Chrysler appear to have made substantial adjust-

Table 3.1   Summary Table for Political Economic Analysis

	Time Horizon		
	Short	Medium	Long
UAW	−	+	−
Ford	0	+	0/−
Chrysler	0	+	0/−
GM	0	+	0/−
Japanese	0	+	+
Consumers	0	−	+

ments over the period of the mid- and late-1980s that have increased their competitiveness vis-à-vis their Japanese competitors. It seems reasonable to conclude that the U.S. industry is somewhat smaller, somewhat more flexible, and somewhat more efficient. One must, however, be careful in evaluating the relationship between international competition, protection, and this improved competitiveness. With or without trade protection these firms would have made the adjustments in output mix, production facilities, and organization of production. It is Japanese competition, not U.S. protection, that accounts for the improvements in performance by the major U.S. auto producers. The Chrysler experience is particularly informative when compared to the VER. In the former case, the publicness of the transfer and the emphasis on the responsibility of the Chrysler Corporation and the UAW for the problems of the firm and the solution to those problems created strong incentives to improve performance. With the VER, the implication that the problem was (probably unfair) competition from abroad created poor incentives to improve performance. Where the Chrysler loan was repaid ahead of schedule, the VER, originally intended as a three-year measure, dragged on for nearly a decade.

Table 3.1 provides a very rough summary of this discussion. The participants are entered in the table roughly in order of their degree of support for trade activism with respect to Japanese auto producers (i.e., both support for the VER and domestic content legislation): the UAW and Ford were the most active supporters, with Chrysler holding back during the early period because of the loan guarantee and the Carter administration's opposition to auto protection; GM opposed protection, but not very actively; and the Japanese producers, and the dealers, opposed protection strongly. Although the consumer interest was not well represented (except perhaps by the dealers), they are included in the table to remind us that they are the source of most of the gains realized by the other participants. Because the restraint was not binding in the immediate post-VER period, only the UAW experienced any effect. As a result of the general economic conditions, the UAW made significant concessions during this period. The other agents in the auto industry experienced essentially no gains as a result of the VER. In the medium term, as the economy recovered and the VER became binding on Japanese firms, all of the active agents gained, while the inactive consumers lost. The evaluation of the long run depends on two factors: how one evaluates the use that was made by the U.S. firms of the period during which the VER was binding, and how one evaluates the effect of increased Japanese investment in the United States. We have argued above that the former effect appears to be small positive to zero, while the latter effect is primarily negative. The entries in the last two cells in the third column primarily reflect the effect of a more competitive domestic market.

3.3   Conclusion: So Why *Did* They Do It?

The U.S. automobile industry sought and received protection from Japanese competition that was not binding in the short run (for reasons that were widely understood at the time) and whose long-run economic effects were, at best, uncertain.[7] The investment of substantial political resources in seeking fairly modest economic gains at a time when there were a variety of more immediately productive government actions that could be sought (e.g., regulatory relief, direct subsidies, relaxation of antitrust enforcement) strongly suggests that something other than simple rent seeking was going on. Specifically, Nelson (1996) argues that the automobile industry was seeking to reestablish a stable, (imperfectly) competitive regime in the U.S. market by using state power to discipline Japanese competitors. That is, in a reversal of the logic applied in much of the economic theory of regulation which sees economic agents seeking economic goals in the political system, the auto industry was seeking a political goal whose object was the economy.

If we refer to the complex set of arrangements that regulate the relations among the various agents that make up the U.S. auto industry as a "sectoral regime," the main institutional members of the regime were the three major producers, the UAW, and the various supplier firms. Local, state, and federal governments are all heavily involved with the regime as well. While it would be wrong to see the auto regime as static, or unconflictual, the basic details of the regime were in place not long after the Second World War. The major attributes of this regime were a stable oligopoly, with GM acting as a price leader, and rent sharing between the firms, the UAW, and, to a lesser extent, the supplier firms. The main source of conflict in the regime was primarily over the distribution of the oligopolistic rents. However, as long as the regime remained fairly stable, such conflicts were relatively minor and well institutionalized. For a variety of reasons, the surging Japanese imports in the mid- and late-1970s could not be managed by the industry (as European imports in the late 1950s and early 1960s had been) and threatened the foundations of the regime. In response, the U.S. industry sought protection not primarily for short-run

7. The uncertainty of the long-run effects derived primarily from the effects on investment in the United States by the Japanese majors and questions about the long-run sustainability of protection.

rent-seeking reasons but as part of an attempt to reconstitute the auto regime on more or less the same terms as had existed prior to the import shock.

Ultimately, however, this political effort to recreate a particular economic order failed. One of the striking things about the auto story is that, while the auto industry got more or less what it wanted from the state, it was the U.S. industry, not the Japanese industry, that did the adjusting. Competition in the auto industry is now global competition. Given international sourcing strategies, multinational investment, joint ventures, and captive imports, even the meaning of a "national" industry has become unclear. The U.S. auto industry's attempt to resist this reality ultimately failed.[8] That is, the protection may have delayed the adjustment by a matter of five or six years, at considerable cost to the consumer, but the result is a global auto regime. The continued viability of GM, Ford, and Chrysler depends on their ability to adjust to this new reality and to participate in the creation of a political-economic regime that does not rely on the policy actions of a single national government, even one as powerful as the United States.[9]

References

Finger, J. M., H. K. Hall, and D. R. Nelson. 1982. The political-economy of administered protection. *American Economic Review* 72, no. 3:452–66.

Hufbauer, G. C., D. Berliner, and K. Elliott. 1986. *Trade protection in the United States.* Washington, D.C.: Institute for International Economics.

Nelson, D. R. 1989. On the high track to protection: The U.S. automobile industry, 1979–1981. In *Pacific dynamics,* ed. S. Haggard and C. Moon, 97–128. Boulder, Colo.: Westview Press.

———. 1996. The political economy of U.S. automobile protection. In *The political economy of American trade policy,* ed. A. O. Krueger. Chicago: University of Chicago Press, forthcoming.

Stigler, G. 1975. Supplementary note on economic theories of regulation. In *The citizen and the state: Essays on regulation,* 137–41. Chicago: University of Chicago Press.

United States International Trade Commission (USITC). 1980. *Certain motor vehicles and certain chassis and bodies therefor: Report to the president on investigation TA-201-44 under Section 201 of the Trade Act of 1974.* USITC Publication no. 1110. Washington, D.C.: GPO.

8. The attempts by the European industry and by Canadian labor to avoid this logic seem increasingly desperate, though both continue to fight the valiant fight.

9. Note that I am not arguing that government intervention has no effect. Quite to the contrary. We have seen in this paper that the effects can be considerable. The point is that in the context of large changes in a complex industrial regime, it is virtually impossible to predict consequences even if control of such a regime were possible.

4   Import Protection for U.S. Textiles and Apparel: Viewed from the Domestic Perspective

J. Michael Finger and Ann Harrison

In the post–World War II era, the U.S. textile and apparel industries achieved a degree of protection that was unparalleled in the rest of the manufacturing sector. Although textiles and apparel together employ less than 2 percent of the total labor force, they account for over 80 percent of the net cost of all import restrictions in the United States (Hufbauer and Elliott 1994). This industry's unusual success in attaining import protection is also evident from the fact that it was the only manufacturing sector to win a multilateral quota arrangement sanctioned by the General Agreement on Tariffs and Trade (GATT).[1]

Our focus in this paper is on the mechanics of domestic protection: on the laws that gave the executive branch the authority to restrict textile imports and on the executive branch's implementation of that authority. We emphasize these dimensions for two reasons: (1) the more visible conflicts between nations over the international agreements to restrict textile and apparel trade have been extensively and skillfully studied, and (2) overlooking the mechanics of how protection was put in place leads one to overlook one of the most powerful actors in the story—the state itself. In determining the scope and magnitude of protection to U.S. textile and garment interests, the U.S. government was more than a neutral intermediary. It was one of the most influential players in the game.

4.1   Winning Protection: The Early Years

During the 1950s, imports of cotton textiles increased rapidly, and by the end of the decade imports accounted for over one-third of the U.S. market in

J. Michael Finger is a lead economist of the International Trade Division of the International Economics Department at The World Bank. Ann Harrison is assistant professor at Columbia University and a faculty research fellow of the National Bureau of Economic Research.

1. In 1955, the U.S. government negotiated a GATT waiver for U.S. agricultural protection.

several important product categories. These import surges prompted inflammatory statements against Japanese exports and an occasional congressional bill to impose quotas or other limits.

There was little chance that such bills would gain approval. The lessons of the Smoot-Hawley tariff were fresh in mind, and Congress was reluctant to take direct action to limit imports. There was even less chance that a protectionist bill could avoid a presidential veto. While Congress perceived trade policy as a means of helping local industry, the executive branch of the U.S. government saw trade policy as an important instrument of foreign policy.

Influenced by Wilsonian ideals of the international rule of law and the populist idea that trading made good neighbors, the executive's approach to trade policy was conditioned by two decades of progress. The executive branch had been in an almost continuous negotiation with its trading partners over trade restrictions. Not just principle but conditioned reflex pushed the executive away from unilateral action on trade restrictions.

Although such direct routes to more protection appeared to be unrealistic in the post–World War II climate, Congress had also created several "administrative" routes to protection. These more indirect avenues for protection gave the president authority to restrict imports under specific circumstances, but left him with the discretionary authority not to do so.[2] These more indirect avenues allowed congressional representatives who faced demands for import protection to direct constituents to the appropriate administrative mechanism.[3]

4.1.1   The Textile Industry's Strategy

The effort to gain protection was led by textile interests, who were more affected by import competition than the apparel industry. Manufacturers of cotton textiles, who were most affected by imports, played a particularly important role. The industry's strategy was the obvious one: to maintain pressure on all political fronts for direct protective measures and at the same time to use all available administrative remedies. On the political front, the industry was active at public hearings concerning the U.S. government's intentions to negotiate tariff reductions under the Reciprocal Trade Agreements Act.

The industry quickly learned that the executive was reluctant to limit imports. In 1955, 1959, and again in 1961, the American Textile Manufacturers

2. Even the Smoot-Hawley tariff provided for such administrative adjustment of tariffs. In a "Section 336" (of the Smoot-Hawley Act) the U.S. Tariff Commission would conduct an investigation to determine the cost of producing a product in the United States and in exporting countries. Based on that information, the Tariff Commission would then recommend to the president the rate change that would "equalize competition," i.e., a tariff rate that would make the foreign cost plus the tariff equal to the domestic cost. Section 336 allowed for tariff reductions as well as for increases. Over the twelve-year life of the section (1930–1941) most petitions for investigations were rejected (256 of 357). In almost half of the times the commission conducted an investigation, it recommended no change of the tariff. Of 101 investigations, 29 led to tariff increases, 25 to reductions.

3. All eighty-one requests by Congress for a Section 336 investigation were honored by the Tariff Commission.

Institute (ATMI) petitioned the secretary of agriculture for broader import quotas under Section 22 of the Agricultural Adjustment Act.[4] The Eisenhower administration exploited the fact that there were no deadlines for a Section 22 investigation and left the 1955 petition tied up in the secretary of agriculture's preliminary investigation. The 1959 and 1961 petitions were thwarted in a different way: the executive (the Eisenhower administration in 1959, the Kennedy administration in 1961) exploited its authority to draft the terms of reference for a Section 22 investigation, and focused the investigations on the impact of imports on the U.S. government's agricultural *export* programs rather than on its domestic price or income support programs. Likewise, when the American Textile Manufacturers Institute asked for quotas on imports of cotton, synthetic fiber, silk, and wool products under the national security provisions of the Trade Agreements Act, the executive took advantage of the absence of a time limit on such investigations and never announced a decision. A 1956 petition for "escape clause" relief came to a similar end, and it became evident that the executive would take advantage of whatever loopholes were available to prevent the trade remedy mechanisms from interfering with a U.S. foreign policy that scorned restrictions on imports.

4.1.2   The Opportunity That Paid Off

By the fall of 1961, the Trade Expansion Act (TEA) had become an important part of President John F. Kennedy's agenda. To President Kennedy and his allies in the government, commercial diplomacy was first of all a tool of foreign policy. Through a new round of GATT negotiations the president could build a relationship with the increasingly successful European Common Market, and thereby renew the strategic alliance between the United States and Western Europe. Though the economics of the argument remained vague, the TEA also became the president's response to pressures for action on the continuing U.S. trade deficit and the gold drain. In addition, the Kennedy administration argued that the act would stimulate the domestic economy: it became something of a panacea for present problems and future circumstances, foreign and domestic.

Yet Kennedy needed support from a powerful southern delegation in Congress to pass the TEA. Textile protection was an issue on which the southern delegation was unified. The textile and apparel industries were by far the largest providers of manufacturing jobs in the South, accounting for over half of total manufacturing employment in several states. During his 1960 campaign, Kennedy pledged to make the cotton textile import problem a top prior-

---

4. Section 22, added to the Agricultural Adjustment Act on August 24, 1935, authorized the president to impose import fees or quotas to restrict imports of agricultural commodities *or the products thereof* if those imports render or tend to render ineffective or materially interfere with U.S. agricultural programs. The section, by design, was similar in scope and purpose to Section 3(e) of the National Industrial Recovery Act (NIRA), which authorized the president to limit imports that interfered with an approved NIRA industry recovery program.

ity of his administration. Based on this pledge, the southern delegation bartered their support for the TEA against protection for the textile and apparel industry. To win their support for the bill, President Kennedy offered a seven-point program for textile and apparel protection. As a key element of this program, the State Department was directed to convene a conference of textile importing and exporting countries to develop an international agreement governing textile trade.

U.S. participation in such negotiations would proceed under the authority granted to the president under Section 204 of the Agriculture Act of 1956. Section 204 authorized the president to negotiate with foreign governments to limit the export to the United States of agricultural *or textile* products, and to carry out such an agreement by limiting the entry of such products into the United States. Before the TEA came to a vote, the southern congressional delegation had pushed through an amendment to Section 204 that would give the president power, once agreement with some countries was in place, to restrict imports from countries *not party* to the agreement.

By March 1962, Kennedy had implemented or made commitments that would soon implement all seven points of his proposed program to help the industry. The Long Term Arrangement on Cotton Textiles, which provided for protection from imports that caused or threatened market disruption, was signed in February 1962. In April 1962, acting under Section 204 authority, Kennedy embargoed eight categories of cotton textile imports from Japan.[5] When the TEA came up for a vote in June 1962, an overwhelming majority of southerners in both the House and the Senate voted for the bill.

4.2   The Origins and Implementation of the Multi-Fibre Arrangement (MFA)

Richard Nixon, running for the presidency in 1968, had learned from Kennedy's experience about the power of the textile industry. He pledged in his campaign to negotiate an international agreement that would include wool and man-made fiber products. After the elections, the Nixon administration used Section 204 to expand the Long Term Arrangement. Section 204, as amended in 1962, provided a powerful weapon to force foreign countries to negotiate limits on their exports to the United States. It put the U.S. government in a position, once agreement had been reached with some countries, to threaten unilateral action against any country reluctant to come to terms. Section 204 also made it difficult for exporting countries to unify to strengthen their negotiating position. After concluding agreements with Hong Kong, South Korea,

---

5. The industry in turn kept its part of the bargain. With these restrictions in place, the National Cotton Council and the American Textile Manufacturers Institute supported the TEA. Two-thirds of Congressman Carl Vinson's Textiles Conference Group voted for the bill and against critical amendments restricting the president's negotiating authority. Eighty-two of 105 House southern Democrats voted for the TEA; in the Senate, 19 of 20 southerners.

and Taiwan, the Nixon administration was in a position to take unilateral action against other exporters, and exporting-country opposition was chipped away.[6] The new agreement, known as the Multi-Fibre Arrangement (MFA), replaced the Long Term Arrangement and extended protection to include both wool and synthetics.[7]

The main operative provision of the Multi-Fibre Arrangement, carried over from the Long Term Arrangement, was Article 3. Article 3 provided that whenever imports of a particular product caused or threatened market disruption, the importing country could request the exporting country to restrict its exports. While the Arrangement specified that the request for restraint be accompanied by a "detailed factual statement of the reasons for the request," it implicitly left to the importing country the authority to determine when "disruption" was present or threatened. Other provisions identified the kinds of restrictions sanctioned under GATT, such as restrictions on products, growth in quotas, and other details.

4.2.1   How Protection Is Administered

Under the MFA, U.S. textile import restraints are administered by the Committee for Implementation of the Textile Agreements (CITA). When the textile industry believes that market disruption is occurring in a particular product category, the industry (usually through its association, the American Textile Manufacturers Institute makes the facts known to CITA. CITA usually meets at the level of deputy assistant secretary (senior civil service), with the Commerce Department representative chairing. CITA then develops its own "disruption statement," on which the industry often comments. Those comments often include the provision of more up-to-date data on the state of the domestic industry, such as data on output, prices, or employment.

If CITA concludes that market disruption is occurring, it issues a "call," a notification to the exporting country that its exports of a particular product are causing market disruption. Following the notification, a preliminary quota is imposed. Under MFA guidelines, the U.S. government then enters into negotiations with the exporting country to agree on a final quota level.

In the end, industry officials insist, there is a loose relation between the disruption statement and the quota level that is set. While the Commerce Department administrators are usually sympathetic to the industry's position, quota levels must win the approval of CITA, which includes two "general interest" departments, State and Treasury. Industry officials insist that even the initial quota is often larger than the limit actually needed to stop market disruption, and that the final level is often more than twice the level of the initial quota. During the first ten months of 1984, when imports surged as the dollar

---

6. Brandis (1982, 43).

7. Richard Nixon, running for the presidency in 1968 against Hubert Humphrey, had learned from the 1960 lesson of the power of the textile industry. He thus pledged in his campaign to negotiate an international agreement that would include wool and man-made fiber products.

appreciated, the ATMI testified that only one-third of the imports of uncontrolled products that were causing market disruption and were eligible for a call under the MFA had in fact been called.

Evidence from the 1980s confirms that the protection received by the industry is porous. Despite the fact that coverage of the MFA expanded significantly during this period, quota utilization rates were, on average, considerably below 100 percent. Quota allocations, which grew at slightly below 6 percent annually in real terms, grew at an even faster pace for some of the major exporters, such as China.

Econometric analysis of the pattern of quota allocation in the United States during the 1980s also shows that market disruption was only one of several factors which affected quota determination. Empirical proxies for market disruption (e.g., import penetration, loss of employment) were significant determinants of which products were under quota, but other factors were important as well. In particular, the faster-growing and richer, industrializing countries were more likely to have quota restraints imposed on their exports, while important markets for U.S. exports were less likely to face quota protection.

4.2.2   Impact of Protection

The degree of protection won by the textile and apparel industries was substantial. Although textiles and apparel account for less than 2 percent of total employment in the U.S. economy, protecting them against import competition accounts for 83 percent of the net cost to the U.S. economy of all import restrictions. Cline (1990) estimates that quotas as of 1986 provided the equivalent of a 28 percent tariff on textiles and a 53 percent tariff on apparel. Even so, imports have continued to capture an increasing share of the U.S. market. When the first international textile arrangement was concluded in the early 1960s, imports accounted for only 5 percent of the U.S. market for textiles, and an even smaller percentage of the U.S. market for apparel. By 1992, textile imports had risen to 20 percent of the U.S. market, while apparel imports accounted for 35 percent.

4.3   Why Protection, Why VERs? Bad Economics

The U.S. textile and apparel industry's case for protection emphasized the loss of jobs and output by U.S. workers and businesses. Resistance to this pressure came from the executive branch of the U.S. government. Although the executive could count on support from U.S. heavy industry and large U.S. banks when it sought authority to negotiate GATT for lower protection, U.S. business provided no direct opposition to textile industry petitions for protection. The auto industry, for example, would support President Kennedy's Trade Expansion Act, but it would not testify at an escape-clause or Section 22 investigation that restrictions on textile exports would increase its costs and thereby endanger jobs in the auto industry.

The political power of southern textile interests, combined with a lack of opposition from other industries, meant that the executive branch was forced to make important concessions to the textile and apparel industries. These concessions were made in spite of the fact that the executive felt that foreign policy interests were best served by a policy of free trade. By the 1990s, however, the balance of power had shifted away from the textile and apparel interests.

In 1994, the U.S. government signed the Uruguay Round Agreement, which provides that all textile and apparel quotas will be eliminated within ten years. Yet this loss by the industry does not reflect any realization by the U.S. voting public or even the U.S. government that protecting textile and apparel products came at a significant cost to U.S. consumers. Rather, it reflects two unrelated factors. First, changes in congressional rules and southern voting patterns diminished the southern delegation's influence. Second, from a mercantilist perspective, support turned against U.S. textile and apparel producers. Textile exporting countries are now valued as markets for services and technology-based products, hence the textile and apparel industry's mercantilist interests were traded for those of other U.S. producers.

Why were voluntary export restraints (VERs) used instead of tariffs? Although a VER is a higher-cost form of protection than a tariff, it was an instrument that accommodated the various influences that came together to shape protection. Pressure for protection from the textile industry was, of course, one of these influences, but there were counterpressures as well. In the 1930s, after the Smoot-Hawley tariff was enacted and other countries had retaliated, governments were wary of triggering further retaliation. Negotiation with the exporting country was the usual response to domestic pressure for increased protection. The success of the Reciprocal Trade Agreements program and the creation under U.S. leadership of GATT intensified the U.S. executive's focus on negotiation as the way of establishing trade policy. Along with these changes came an increased reluctance to limit U.S. imports, even through negotiations. Under pressure, however, the executive would turn to the VER. A negotiated VER minimized the "costs" of protection—it minimized harm to the foreign policy "relationship" that existed between the United States and the exporting country.

References

Brandis, R. Buford. 1982. *The making of textile trade policy 1935–1981.* Washington, D.C.: American Textile Manufacturers Institute.

Cline, William R. 1990. *The future of world trade in textiles and apparel.* Rev. ed. Washington, D.C.: Institute for International Economics.

Hufbauer, Gary Clyde, and Kimberly Ann Elliott. 1994. *Measuring the costs of protection in the United States.* Washington, D.C.: Institute for International Economics.

5   Do Precedent and Legal Argument Matter in the Lumber CVD Cases?

Joseph P. Kalt

5.1   Rational Political Economy and U.S.-Canadian Lumber Disputes

Efforts by interested parties to secure trade protection are frequently carried out in the United States through the quasi-judicial regulatory framework of countervailing duty (CVD) law, as administered by the Department of Commerce (DoC). Parties who participate in the department's litigation process, however, often confess to perceptions that the process is a charade; the hearings and filings before the department's International Trade Administration (ITA) and International Trade Commission (ITC) have no influence on the ultimate policy outcomes. Instead, it is averred, the policy outcomes are driven by interest group politics, leaving the litigatory apparatus to serve merely as beside-the-fact packaging for decisions made elsewhere and through different, "purely political" processes.

This paper tries to get at the questions of whether and how the quasi-judicial regulatory process by which CVD law is administered affects the success or failure of parties petitioning for protection. The ongoing dispute between the United States and Canada over trade in lumber and logs serves as the context.[1] The "timber trade war" centers on claims by U.S. milling interests that the Canadians provide publicly owned trees to loggers at subsidized prices, and that Canadian log export restraints subsidize the prices that Canadian sawmills pay for raw logs.

This research focuses on the role that a particular legal institution—*legal*

Joseph P. Kalt is the Ford Foundation Professor of International Political Economy at the John F. Kennedy School of Government at Harvard University and served as an economic consultant to the governments of Canada and British Columbia in the Lumber III trade dispute.

The author has benefited greatly from access to the documentary record in the proceedings of the Canadian Lumber III trade dispute. Any errors or omissions are his, as are the preliminary views set forth.

1. See Kalt (1988).

precedent—plays in determining the successes and failures of the contending parties as they tussle over such matters as the applicability of CVD law. Legal precedent is treated as a costly barrier that litigants face when trying to exert political influence. Resources are expended by competing parties to defend or break down precedents in a stochastic process of "take your best shot (via legal argument) and hope you hit the bull's-eye." What arguments work and why?

At some risk of caricature, economic theories of rational political economy are currently pulling scholars into two broad camps: Capture Theory (CT) and the New Institutionalism (NI). Under the former, it is argued that political outcomes can be explained by a combination of two primary economic factors: (1) the differential stakes that contending parties have in a particular law or regulation, that is, where the rents are; and (2) the differential costs of effective political organization that contending rent-seeking interest groups confront as a result of standard Olsonian forces of free riding.[2] Within this framework, regulatory outcomes and processes are "captured" by successful interest groups who wield the most effective political influence, where "influence" is usually measured either by votes delivered to politicians or votes plus campaign contributions delivered to politicians.

The New Institutionalism does not deny that the two primary factors underlying CT are indeed important (if not strictly "primary"), but adds a third fundamental explanatory factor to efforts to understand political outcomes. This factor is the institutional context—laws, procedures, precedents, regulations, voting rules, and so on—that forms the playing field upon which contending rent seekers meet. NI lays claim to every bit as much economic rationality in the modeling of political actors as does CT, but argues that institutional structure constitutes binding constraints, or at least conditioning costs, that limit the range of actors' investments in political outcomes and hence play determinative roles in political outcomes.[3]

As these theories play out in the investigation of a particular class of political action, such as decisions of the ITA regarding trade protection for U.S. lumber interests, they carry testably different implications. According to CT, institutions such as legal proceedings are "Stiglerian theater"; the real game is being played out behind the scenes of the hearing rooms by interest groups and support-maximizing politicians.[4] Legal rulings and such matters as precedent may be a language by which the game is explained or justified after the fact to appease the press and the public, but they are not determinative of outcomes. NI would hold, however, that such institutions as precedent, standards of evidence, and burdens of proof *matter;* agency decision makers and judges can't simply ignore precedent, evidence, or procedure no matter how much political

2. The classic statements here are from the Chicago School: Stigler (1971), Peltzman (1976), Becker (1983).

3. See, e.g., North (1990), Bates (1988), and the writings of the "rational political economists."

4. The nature of such support maximization is worked out for the case of no principal-agent slack by, e.g., Peltzman (1976) and Becker (1983).

vailing duty rate for Canadian lumber imports at 14.5 percent ad valorem. The Lumber II CVD was effectively preempted, however, when escalating retaliatory threats by the Canadians compelled the United States and Canada to enter into a Memorandum of Understanding (MOU). The Lumber II MOU obligated Canada to impose a 15 percent fee on softwood lumber exports to the United States.[6]

In 1991, Canada and a number of its provinces concluded that the MOU had been satisfied and lifted the 15 percent export fee. The DoC's ITA immediately launched Lumber III to investigate whether Canadian stumpage policies continued to constitute a countervailable subsidy. At the invitation of the ITA, the Coalition for Fair Lumber Imports filed submissions arguing that Canada's log export restraints (LERs) also constitute a countervailable subsidy.[7] On Final Determination in 1992, the ITA found both Canadian stumpage and LERs to be countervailable and set an ad valorem CVD of 6.51 percent for lumber imported into the United States from Alberta, British Columbia, Ontario, and Quebec. As of 1994, the Final Determination was subject to ongoing appeal before a binational panel created pursuant to the recent U.S.-Canada free trade agreement.

The stakes in the lumber dispute are large. Duties on the order of 5 percent to 15 percent translate into hundreds of millions of dollars annually. Lumber II, for example, concerned only stumpage, yet it has been estimated that its CVD would have produced (i.e., but for the MOU) tariff revenues of more than $340 million per year for the United States, and net gains for U.S. lumber producers of more than $400 million per year.[8] In the case of Lumber III, the duties set forth by the ITA's Final Determination would offset alleged subsidies totaling more than $390 million per year.

These stakes obviously motivate the contending parties. The tariff-seeking interests throughout Lumber I, II, and III have consisted of medium and smaller U.S. logging and milling operations organized as the Coalition for Fair Lumber Imports, joined with force by at least one of the very large U.S. operators (Georgia Pacific Corporation), and orchestrated by a U.S. law firm renowned for lobbying and legal efforts on behalf of protection-seeking parties. A number of large U.S.-based operators, such as Weyerhauser, have been expanding their investments in Canada. This apparently has tended to cool any enthusiasm for CVD action against Canadian lumber imports. U.S. lumber consumers (who stand to lose from tariffs on Canadian lumber) have largely been inactive in the lumber dispute. The active opposition to CVD action has consistently come from Canadian sawmills and the Canadian government. In particular, participation in the legal proceedings has primarily been led and

---

6. See Kalt (1988) for a discussion and calculation of the international welfare effects of Lumber II.

7. Ironically, since Lumber II, the United States had tightened log export restrictions of its own—aimed at stemming log exports across the Pacific.

8. See Kalt (1988).

Table 5.1   **Hypothetical Boolean Summary Table (upper case = presence; lower case = absence)**

Y = Win, y = Lose	Factor—A or a	Factor—B or b
Y	a	B
Y	A	B

financed by the provincial forestry ministries. Canadian mill operators have cooperated with their governmental agents.

5.3   Boolean Representation of the Legal Arguments in Lumber III

The tariff-seeking U.S. interests have been the most influential party in Lumber III, in the sense that they have won their case before the ITA—but this does not explain why they won. As noted, I use the Boolean pseudoregression techniques pioneered by Ragin to investigate the factors that might explain what makes a winning argument in the Lumber III CVD proceedings before the ITA.[9] Boolean analysis proceeds by coding an outcome of interest for dichotomous results. In the case at hand, the outcome of an argument is coded Win or Lose. Possible explanatory factors in determining when an outcome (e.g., Win) occurs are coded for their presence or absence. The resulting coding can be represented by a table of the kind illustrated above.

Boolean analysis describes the outcome in the first case (row) as $Y = aB$. The second case is coded as $Y = AB$. Multiplication in Boolean analysis is read as "and," while addition is read as "or." Thus, we can say that $Y = aB + AB$; that is, Y occurs when either a and B are present together or A and B are present together. If this is a well-specified model of the factors explaining Y, $Y = aB + AB$ can be further reduced by factoring to $Y = B(a + A) = B$. In other words, B is a necessary and sufficient condition to cause Y, and it doesn't matter whether A is present or not. More generally, necessary and sufficient conditions are reflected as

$Y = B$	B is both necessary and sufficient;
$Y = A + B$	A and B are each sufficient, but not necessary;
$Y = AB$	Both A and B are necessary, but not sufficient;
$Y = A(B+C)$	A is necessary, but not sufficient.

The coding of "left-hand-side" variables in a case such as the Lumber III Final Determination entails identifying the objective "winner" of a particular argument in the proceeding, as this is indicated in the actual ITA decision. The

9. See Ragin (1987).

explanatory factors (coded for presence or absence with upper and lower case designations) are (from NI)

1. precedent (P/p): precedent on one's side increases the likelihood of winning;

2. straightforward theory (T/t): a coherent, straightforward theory (e.g., an economic reasoning or theory) improves the likelihood of winning;

3. evidence (E/e): having the preponderance of evidence increases the likelihood of winning;

4. ease of exposition (X/x): the likelihood of winning an argument increases with the ease with which it can be communicated;

and (from CT)

5. stakes (S/s): the likelihood of the more influential party winning increases with the stakes at issue in the argument (with the success of U.S. interests in Lumber III making them the most influential party).

I have coded the foregoing factors for a set of fourteen actual arguments from Lumber III. This coding and the winning party in each argument are set forth in table 5.2. The basic assertions of the fourteen arguments are[10]

1. Rent theory: Canadians assert that any below-market stumpage is inframarginal and does not affect lumber production.

2. LER as subsidy: the DoC/CFLI asserts that LERs lower log prices to Canadian millers.

3. Market distortion: Canadians assert that LERs merely offset other countries' (especially Japan's) distortive trade policies.

4. LER price change: Canadians assert that any effect of LERs on log prices must be measured relative to the no-LERs equilibrium, rather than current U.S.-Canadian price differences.

5. General equilibrium effects—existence: Canadians assert that general equilibrium effects that offset log price effects of LERs must be accounted for.

6. General equilibrium effects—measurement: Canadians assert that general equilibrium effects significantly offset log price effects of LERs.

7. Causation tests: Canadians assert that the DoC/CFLI has the burden of demonstrating empirically a "direct and discernible" impact of the LERs on Canadian sawmillers' costs.

8. Other provinces: Canadians assert that LERs in provinces other than British Columbia are not economically binding.

9. Law of One Price: DoC/CFLI asserts that observed differences between U.S. and Canadian prices demonstrate the subsidizing effect of LERs.

10. Relevant market/1: Canadians assert that any price effect of LERs does not "ripple" uniformly from exportable logs across all log types and the entire province of British Columbia.

---

10. I merely state the assertions here. No opinion is expressed regarding the validity of the arguments.

Table 5.2   **Boolean Summary of the Attributes of Observed Winning Arguments in the U.S.-Canadian Lumber Dispute (affirmative = 1; otherwise = 0)**

Issue	Winner	Precedent Favors Winner P = 1; p = 0	Large Stakes S = 1; s = 0	Applicable Theory Is Straightforward T = 1; t = 0	Evidence Favors Winner E = 1; e = 0	Winner's Ease of Exposition X = 1; x = 0
Rent theory	DoC/CFLI	0	1	0	0	1
Log export restraint as subsidy	DoC/CFLI	0	1	0	0	0
Market distortion	DoC/CFLI	0	1	1	0	1
Log export restraint price change	Canada	1	0	1	1	1
General equilibrium effects—existence	Canada	1	0	1	1	1
General equilibrium effects—measurement	DoC/CFLI	0	1	0	0	0
Causation tests	DoC/CFLI	0	1	0	0	0
Other provinces	Canada	1	0	1	1	1
Law of One Price	DoC/CFLI	0	1	0	0	1
Relevant market/1	Canada	1	1	0	0	0
Relevant market/2	DoC/CFLI	0	0	0	0	1
Export preparation costs	DoC/CFLI	1	0	0	0	1
Transport costs	Canada	1	0	1	1	1
Company exclusions	Canada	1	0	1	1	1

11. Relevant market/2: Canadians assert that the ITA erred in Preliminary Determination by assuming a uniform "ripple" of LER price effects across all logs in British Columbia.

12. Export preparation costs: Canadians assert that any comparison between foreign and domestic log prices must be adjusted for costs of preparing logs for export.

13. Transport costs: Canadians assert that transport costs should be deducted from foreign-derived log prices in any attempt to determine no-LER equilibrium prices in domestic British Columbian markets.

14. Company exclusions: Canadians assert that individual mills can be exempted if they are not affected by the alleged subsidy (e.g., do not use British Columbian logs).

Upon factoring table 5.2 (per above), the resulting designation of a winning argument is Win $= pSt + PsX[tE + Te]$. In words this says that

> a winning argument before the ITA has either precedent running against it (p) and a complicated theory (t) but large stakes (S); or precedent in its favor (P), low stakes (s), and easy exposition (X), and either a combination of a complicated theory (t) but strongly supportive evidence (E) or a simple theory (T) albeit weak evidence (e).

Closer inspection of the process of factoring and reduction that produces the prime implicant for Win above reveals that the cases in table 5.2 that produce the first term (pSt) in Win entirely are cases in which the DoC/CFLI is the winning party. Similarly, the cases that produce the second term in Win (i.e., $PsX[tE + Te]$) entirely are cases in which the Canadians are the winners of the argument. From this observation come the key findings of this study:

DoC/CFLI Wins $= pSt$ and Canadians Win $= PsX[tE + Te]$.

To interpret these results, consider the above expression for "DoC/CFLI Wins." The p in pSt represents the absence of supporting precedent for the position taken by the winning party. It is only reasonably interpreted as an impediment to winning an argument. The same interpretation applies to t—the absence of a straightforward theory behind the position taken on the winner's argument. In short, p and t impede the ability of the DoC/CFLI to win an argument. Yet, when the stakes are large (S), the DoC/CFLI wins anyway. We cannot quite say that no matter which institutional factors (i.e., p, t, x, and/or e) run against the DoC/CFLI, the group wins when the stakes are large; the sample of issues in table 5.2 does not include cases in which the DoC/CFLI wins or loses with large S and x and/or e running against it. Nevertheless, it can be said that in the cases available none occur in which institutional aspects of ITA proceedings block a DoC/CFLI win if the stakes in the matter are large.

This last observation *is* the prediction of Capture Theory. It says, contrary to the New Institutionalism, that at least in the cases represented here, no evidence is found that large stakes will not permit the influential, capturing party from overwhelming institutional blockades such as the absence of supportive precedent or the absence of a noncomplicated theory for one's argument. The New Institutionalism is not wholly rejected, however. While the DoC/CFLI has succeeded in Lumber III in securing the ITA's support for tariff protection against Canadian forest products, the Canadian parties have won some arguments along the way. In so doing they have tempered the level of protection successfully sought before the ITA by the DoC/CFLI. As noted above, the second term in "Win" arises from cases in which the Canadian parties prevail in their legal arguments before the ITA, and the Canadian parties win arguments when $PsX[tE + Te]$. Imposing on this expression the priors that neither complicated theories (t) nor weak evidence (e) assists the Canadians in winning the argument, the prime implicant for Canadians Win reduces to

$$\text{Canadians Win} = PsX[tE + Te] = PsX[E + T].$$

This result says that, within the sample of cases encompassed by table 5.2, if the Canadians are to win arguments before the ITA, they require not only issues for which the stakes are small (s), but also institutional help in the form of supportive precedent (P), easy exposition (X), and either strong evidence (E) or a straightforward theory (T). Apparently, the Canadians do not need to have everything in their favor (i.e., $PsXET$) to win an argument before the ITA. Yet even when the issue is a matter with small stakes, they need a considerable array of institutional factors on their side in order to win (i.e., P, X, and E or T).

References

Bates, R. 1988. Contra-contractarianism: Some thoughts on the new institutionalism. *Politics and Society* 16:387–401.

Becker, G. 1983. Competition among pressure groups for political influence. *Quarterly Journal of Economics,* August, 371–98.

Kalt, J. 1988. The political economy of protectionism: Tariffs and retaliation in the timber industry. In *Trade policy issues and empirical analysis,* ed. R. Baldwin, 339–64. Chicago: University of Chicago Press.

North, D. 1990. *Institutions, institutional change, and economic performance.* Cambridge: Cambridge University Press.

Peltzman, S. 1976. Toward a more general theory of regulation. *Journal of Law and Economics,* August, 211–40.

Ragin, Charles C. 1987. *The comparative method.* Berkeley: University of California Press.

Stigler, G. 1971. The economic theory of regulation. *Bell Journal of Economics,* spring, 3–21.

6 The Political Economy of the Export Enhancement Program for Wheat

Bruce L. Gardner

U.S. agriculture faced severe economic problems in the early 1980s. The problems are apparent in the data on farm income and the farm sector's balance sheet. Real farm income (including government assistance) in 1980–84 averaged about half of its level of the period before the commodity boom in the 1970s. The U.S. Department of Agriculture's (USDA) estimate of farm equity, the value of farm assets minus liabilities, declined from $1.14 trillion (1987 dollars) at the end of 1980 to roughly half of that value, $0.6 trillion on January 1, 1985. U.S. wheat growers were among the hardest hit.

The economic problems of wheat growers were addressed in several ways, some of which caused more problems than they solved. The price paid to farmers for wheat placed in government ownership was increased to $4.00 per bushel for the 1982 crop. It had been only $1.37 up to 1975. U.S. wheat acreage planted expanded 45 percent, from 59 million acres in 1973 to 86 million acres in 1982, and the USDA increased its wheat stocks to over a billion bushels in 1982, the highest level since the early 1960s. In reaction, the Payment in Kind (PIK) program was introduced and idled 30 million acres of wheat base in 1983, the largest supply control effort ever. In 1984, direct payments to wheat growers rose to exceed $1.5 billion. Yet none of these measures was capable of stemming the decline in income and equity values through 1985. Because weak export demand was a key element of wheat's economic problems, it was natural to look to export promotion as an additional policy tool.

Bruce L. Gardner is professor of agricultural and resource economics at the University of Maryland, College Park. He is a former assistant secretary for economics in the U.S. Department of Agriculture.

6.1   The Birth of the Export Enhancement Program

In 1983 the Reagan administration, after debate settled only at the cabinet level, accepted the idea of ad hoc subsidized exports of Commodity Credit Corporation (CCC)-owned wheat to targeted North African markets where European Community (EC) wheat was being sold with the help of their export subsidies. This was intended to serve the dual purpose of reducing excessive stock levels and retaliating against EC export subsidies. This venture was a substantial political success, affording an opportunity to attack the EC, please farmers, and hold off congressional pressure for more sweeping programs. The impetus was thus established that led eventually to the full-fledged Export Enhancement Program (EEP).

In Congress, the idea of legislation to target in-kind export subsidies at the EC did not prevail when it was first seriously considered in 1983. The principal reason given by opponents was the worry that such legislation would trigger a trade war in which the EC would increase their subsidies and perhaps withdraw previously negotiated concessions such as their duty-free binding on U.S. oilseed products and feed grain substitutes. In addition, the secretary of agriculture already possessed sufficient authorities for ad hoc export subsidies as needed for surplus commodity management or strategic purposes.

Two years later, as the 1985 farm bill deliberations began, the situation was different in two respects: farm groups had refined their general support for export promotion to more concrete proposals, and U.S. wheat exports had declined still further while the EC's grew. In this situation the administration's desire to continue ad hoc export subsidies without binding legislation was no longer politically tenable.

Senator Robert Dole (R-Kansas) took the lead in organizing a series of meetings in the spring of 1985 to get the Reagan administration to establish a targeted export subsidy program focused on grains, especially wheat. Representatives of the wheat growers as well as other farm groups attended these meetings in Dole's office. In May 1985, the administration (represented by the Office of Management and Budget [OMB] and the USDA) and the Senate leadership (principally Dole and Senator Edward Zorinsky [D-Nebraska]) agreed to implement, under existing USDA authorities, an Export Enhancement Program.

Politically, the EEP was given the breath of life by a conjunction of interests represented by three individuals: Senator Zorinsky's strong desire, as the ranking Democrat on the agriculture committee and representative of Nebraska, for a substantial export subsidy program; budget director David Stockman's need for Democratic votes on key economic legislation; and Senator Dole's brokering savvy, with interests in supporting both the administration (as majority leader) and Kansas wheat growers. Stockman agreed that the administration would implement an export subsidy program, in exchange for Zorinsky's vote on the budget resolution containing the Reagan administration's fiscal proposals, with the subsidies to take the form of unwanted CCC surplus commodities with a zero budget score.

The agreed-upon program committed $2 billion worth of CCC-owned commodities to be made available as a bonus to U.S. exporters to expand sales of U.S. agricultural commodities in targeted markets. The objectives stated were to increase U.S. farm exports and to encourage trading partners to begin serious negotiations on agricultural trade problems.

Guidelines for the EEP, established by the Economic Policy Council of the White House, were that each subsidized sale should meet the following criteria: (1) additionality, that is, net increase in export sales caused by the subsidized sale; (2) targeting to displace competing exporters who are subsidizing their sales; (3) a net gain to the U.S. economy; and (4) budget neutrality. Each proposed EEP initiative was to be tested against these criteria by an interdepartmental committee chaired by the U.S. Trade Representative and the USDA that included representatives from the OMB, the Council of Economic Advisers (CEA), the departments of Treasury, State, Labor, and Commerce, and the National Security Council (NSC). It was never publicly stated how the "net gain to the U.S. economy" and "budget neutrality" criteria were to be defined and measured. Participants in the process indicated that criterion (3) was not a factor in interagency debate, although (1), (2), and (4) were.

The Food Security Act as finally enacted in December 1985 codified the EEP essentially as the administration had established it six months earlier. The main issues, as often in enabling legislation, were what the executive branch "shall" (be required to) do and "may" (has discretionary authority to) do. The 1985 act required the secretary of agriculture to provide CCC commodities at no cost to "United States exporters, users, and processors and foreign purchasers," and required that a total of $2 billion in CCC commodities be used for this purpose during the three fiscal years ending September 30, 1988. The purposes the subsidized exports were to serve are broadly stated: in addition to combating other countries' subsidies and the high value of the dollar, export subsidies may be used to offset "the adverse effects of U.S. agricultural price support levels that are temporarily above the export prices offered by overseas competitors in export markets" (*Food Security Act of 1985, U.S. Statutes at Large* 99:1483).

In addition, the act authorized the unlimited use of cross-subsidization, that is, the use of one CCC commodity to subsidize the export of another. This was politically important because many commodity interests, including processed products and products which did not have price support programs, prevailed upon the agriculture committees for support. Egg producers and pork producers, for example, testified that they needed assistance in competing with EC export subsidies. But no CCC stocks of these commodities existed. The legislation shared EEP benefits across commodities by permitting CCC wheat stocks to be used to subsidize egg or pork exports.

The EEP was not subject to discipline in the annual appropriations process, because the farm support programs are "entitlements"—the appropriations committees provide open-ended funding for the Commodity Credit Corporation to achieve its price support mandates. The committees do not control how the CCC uses its acquired commodity stocks. Congress could have brought budgetary disciplines to bear by scoring EEP costs in Budget Committee proceedings. However, Congress agreed with the OMB on zero scoring for the EEP. The principal argument was that CCC commodities cost so much to store that it was worth as much to give them away as to keep them. In addition, to the extent that increased exports increased the U.S. market price, deficiency payments for wheat and other target-price commodities would be reduced.

The Export Enhancement Program came into being with very little opposition. Why was the way so clear? The natural opponents of an export subsidy are U.S. domestic wheat buyers and foreign wheat producers. In the case of the EEP, U.S. millers were diverted by their participation in subsidized flour exports and by the release of CCC stocks to pay the subsidies. The bakers and broader consumer groups were relatively weak participants, and their participation in the 1985 farm bill debate was focused on opposition to acreage controls and on limiting budgetary outlays. In summary, the Export Enhancement Program was enacted in 1985 because wheat growers and exporters asked for it, and no interest group opposed it, except some economists in general terms. Because the pressure to assist agriculture was strong, and was countered only by budgetary pressures, the OMB finding that the EEP would be budget neutral ensured its supporters of an easy political victory.

6.2 Consequences and Evaluation of the Program

Questions were being raised about the effectiveness of the Export Enhancement Program even before its legislative enactment. The administration announced its first EEP initiatives in May 1985. By October only two sales had been made. In October and November the House Committee on Agriculture's Subcommittee on Department Operations, Research, and Foreign Agriculture held hearings to review complaints about EEP administration.

The procedures for implementing the EEP were far from clear. There were (and are) two main steps: administration approval of an EEP initiative, and the USDA's acceptance of exporters' bids for bonuses under the initiative. The approach raises questions of how the USDA can determine, for each proposed sale, what the competitor's price is. Wouldn't the competitor's price itself be affected by an EEP? And is there sufficient incentive for U.S. commercial exporters to obtain the highest possible market price?

Statistics of EEP shipments are shown in table 6.1. After a slow start, EEP exports reached 26.6 million metric tons in fiscal 1988, about half of all U.S. wheat exports. The average subsidy reached $38 per ton in 1987. A price wedge this large on substantial quantities would be expected to make a noticeable difference in world trade flows and prices.

Table 6.1   **Export Enhancement Program (EEP) Wheat Sales and Bonuses**

Fiscal Year	EEP Sales Metric Tons (millions)	Total EEP Bonus Dollars (millions)	Average EEP Bonus $/mt	Total U.S. Exports[a] Metric Tons (millions)	EEP Share[b] (%)
1985	.5	11	21.84	28.0	2
1986	4.8	126	26.20	20.7	23
1987	14.1	541	38.33	28.1	50
1988	26.6	819	30.83	40.6	66
1989	16.0	288	18.05	37.6	43
1990	14.3	241	16.84	33.2	43
1991	17.7	767	43.18	26.7	67
1992	19.7	813	41.14	34.3	58
1993	21.6	1281	33.82		

Source: Economic Research Service, USDA.

[a]Fiscal year exports, which differ from crop-year data used elsewhere in this paper. Constructed from USDA monthly export statistics.

[b]EEP tonnage as percentage of total export tonnage.

The USDA uses a wheat simulation model in which each million-ton increase in wheat exports generates an increase of ten cents per bushel in the U.S. farm price of wheat. Each ten-cent rise in the price of wheat reduces deficiency payments by $174 million. Empirical studies suggest that an EEP of 20 million tons adds 2 to 6 million tons to U.S. export demand. With a $50 per ton bonus level, the budget outlays for the EEP are $1 billion annually (recent levels). The 2 to 6 million ton increase in exports causes the wheat price to rise twenty to sixty cents per bushel and hence budget outlays to decline $350 to $1,050 million annually. Thus, if the high end of "additionality" pertains, which is what the USDA assumes, the EEP is budget neutral.

The main losses from the Export Enhancement Program accrue to domestic buyers of U.S. wheat. The exact incidence on the buyers' side—among farmers who feed wheat, millers, bakers, retailers, and final consumers—has not been estimated. Because domestic final demand for foods containing wheat is quite inelastic, domestic consumption of these products is unlikely to change appreciably because of the EEP, and in fact domestic use has been quite stable over time despite large changes in wheat prices. It is therefore unlikely that the EEP reduced the demand for, and thus the returns earned by, processors, distributors, or other middlemen. Certainly the evidence in the political debate is consistent with this conclusion. Millers and bakers who took public positions favored the Export Enhancement Program (usually because they had export as well as domestic interests).

Each increase of ten cents per bushel in the price of wheat raises farm income by $60 million and reduces consumers' surplus by $120 million (Salathe 1991). The consumer cost estimate assumes that farm price increases for all

Table 6.2   Economic Gains from the Export Enhancement Program (EEP)

Additionality	.1	.3
	Millon Dollars Annually	
Cost of EEP subsidies	−1000	−1000
Deficiency payment reduction	350	1050
Subtotal: budgetary gain	−650	50
Crop producers' income gain	120	300
Livestock feeders' gain	−40	−100
Consumers' gain	−200	−500
Total U.S. gain	−770	−250

Source: Salathe (1991) and calculations described in text.

domestically used wheat are passed on to consumers without any change in the farm-to-consumer markup or profits in the wheat processing industry. The farm income increase is only about one-fourth of the rise in the market value of the wheat crop because three-fourths of wheat production are protected by deficiency payments which decline cent for cent as the market price rises.

The overall domestic welfare effect of the EEP can be estimated by summing the budget, consumer, and producer changes if we assume that the farm income change is a change in economic rents (i.e., farmland and farm operator labor taken as fixed in supply). For the range of additionality of 0.1 to 0.3, the EEP, at its average recent size of about 20 million tons and cost of $1 billion annually, generates the results shown in table 6.2. While an optimistic assumption of additionality permits the EEP to achieve the objective of budget neutrality, no assumption permits the program to achieve its cost-effectiveness objective of providing a benefit to the U.S. economy. Indeed, by these estimates the EEP is a particularly inefficient income transfer program, generating almost $1 in deadweight losses (from the U.S. viewpoint) for each $1 of farm income gain even under an optimistic additionality assumption. The main reason for the large net U.S. losses is that so much of the subsidy is a transfer to foreign buyers of U.S. wheat.

6.3   Political Response to the EEP in the 1990s

In 1990 the legislation authorizing the EEP (and other farm programs) expired and was reconsidered in a comprehensive set of hearings (U.S. House 1991; U.S. Senate 1991). This provided a convenient opportunity for interest groups to express second thoughts and to suggest modifications of the EEP. The National Association of Wheat Growers, as well as representatives of other commodities using the program, were totally supportive of continuation of the EEP without substantial change. Concerns that had been expressed in the 1985 House hearings about targeting as opposed to a generally available subsidy disappeared. Grain users might have been expected to be more critical, but more of them supported the EEP in 1990 than in 1985. The American Bakers Association, the Biscuit and Cracker Manufacturers' Association, and the North American Export Grain Association all testified in favor of continuing the program.

Because of firm support from commodity and agribusiness groups, and weak opposition, the EEP emerged unchanged in structure and strengthened in budget in the 1990 Farm Act. EEP spending was far higher in fiscal 1991 through 1993 than in any previous three-year period (table 6.1). The solid political support was attributable not so much to particular export achievements of the EEP, but to farmers' general satisfaction with the recovery of farm income from mid-1980s lows and the role of the commodity programs in that recovery. CCC wheat inventories had been sold off, deficiency payments protected producers from low prices in 1986, the export market had recovered with the dollar's decline from its 1985 high, and reduced output boosted wheat prices back to 1980–81 levels in 1989 and 1990. Farm interests in the 1990 farm bill debate were devoted mainly to attempting to forestall the budget cuts (about $2 billion annually) that the Bush administration was calling for. The EEP was thus seen as a piece of a set of programs that were working.

Beyond general satisfaction with the situation, EC subsidized exports remained a principal threat to U.S. grain producers. The EEP was seen as particularly valuable in this situation, with the Uruguay Round languishing in its fifth year of negotiations. The 1990 act authorized the EEP at a level of not less than $500 million annually and explicitly authorized cash as well as in-kind subsidies. It said that the only purpose of the EEP was "to discourage unfair trade practices" (U.S. House 1990, 335). The context for this focus was the continued expansion of the European Community's subsidized exports and the EC's intransigence on agriculture in the Uruguay Round, then scheduled for completion in December 1990. The Omnibus Budget Reconciliation Act, enacted in October 1990 along with the Farm Act, contained a "GATT trigger" that required spending $1 billion annually on the EEP if no Uruguay Round agreement had been reached by June 30, 1992. (Since it turned out that no agreement was reached by that time, EEP spending duly proceeded at about the $1 billion rate.)

Opposition to the EEP in 1990 was mitigated because farm bill reformers focused on other policies. The only organized reform effort, by a coalition of conservative Republicans and urban Democrats in the House of Representatives, brought to the floor of the House amendments to reduce or eliminate the sugar, wool, and honey programs, and eliminate deficiency payments to farms with over a million dollars in sales or farmers who earned more than $100,000 from off-farm sources. The amendments all failed. They had more apparent popular appeal than an anti-EEP amendment would have; this helps explain why none was offered.

A second important factor mitigating opposition to the EEP was its continuing to be scored as budget neutral. The reforms that were successful in 1990, most notably the introduction of a 15 percent reduction in deficiency payments by making 15 percent of each producer's base acreage ineligible for payments, were driven by the budget reconciliation agreement to cut $13 billion from farm program spending over the five fiscal years 1992 through 1996.[1] The $1 billion annual spending on the EEP would have been a prime target for cuts if the program had not been scored as budget neutral by the OMB.

Finally, it is noteworthy that the EC has introduced significant reforms of the Common Agricultural Policy (CAP), including acreage set-aside and other measures to reduce outlays on their export subsidies, and that the permanence of these reforms has been strengthened by the General Agreement on Tariffs and Trade (GATT) on agriculture reached in January 1994. This agreement requires that both Europe and the United States reduce export subsidies substantially over a five-year period. The United States's willingness to spend on the EEP quite likely had a role in encouraging these reforms, though how important a role is unclear.[2]

6.4   Conclusions

Interest-group outcomes of the EEP can be summarized as follows. Wheat producers were substantial economic gainers from the program. Wheat exporting businesses were also supportive of the EEP, and were winners. Other agricultural producers, notably, feed grains, gained by obtaining a piece of the EEP action and also supported the program. The losing groups—domestic grain processors and consumers—did not visibly oppose the program.

Perhaps the most striking feature of the political economy of the Export Enhancement Program is how little impact standard economic arguments have had. Economists have produced many analyses showing that the program, even as a second-best measure, generates a net loss to the U.S. economy.

The biggest losers from the Export Enhancement Program are buyers of

---

1. This cut was calculated from a five-year baseline of future spending, not from current (1990) levels. As it turned out, farm program spending was not $13 billion below the 1990 baseline. Indeed, the cuts notwithstanding, farm program spending between 1992 and 1995 has exceeded the baseline level that was projected *before* the "13 billion cut."

2. Although it is even more conjectural than the earlier calculations, CAP reform and GATT could well reduce EC wheat exports by 3 to 4 million tons annually and raise the U.S. market price by twenty to thirty cents per bushel. The resulting gain for U.S. producers would be $120 to $180 million annually, and the gains to taxpayers would be $350 to $520 million (because of fewer deficiency payments). U.S. consumers would lose $240 to $360 million. The overall net gain to the United States, roughly equal to the price increase times wheat exports, would be $230 to $350 million.

Suppose the EEP accelerated CAP reform by five years. Then the EEP generated $1.1 to $1.8 billion for the United States. The overall U.S. cost of the EEP between 1990 and 1992 was $510 million annually, or about $2 to $3 billion between 1986 and 1993. These calculations are of course crude, but they indicate that it is quite difficult to obtain any net U.S. gain from the EEP as a strategic investment, even under the assumption that it successfully induced policy changes in the EC.

wheat, with losses of $250 to $600 million per year according to estimates presented earlier, with recent world price data suggesting that the lower end of the range is more likely. But no buyers of wheat—millers, bakers, livestock producers, or consumers of retail products containing wheat—have raised politically significant objections to the program. Agribusiness interests probably did not bear any losses. Livestock feeders' costs have not been substantial, and a feeling of solidarity along with logrolling keeps them from opposing the program. Consumer costs are only about $1 to $3 per year per person, and the general public remains generally supportive of farmers according to polls.

In short, the Export Enhancement Program has proved a political winner because

- wheat producers see a benefit from it;
- wheat producers have a unified view on the issue, and they have effective channels of influence through the congressional Agriculture committees;
- wheat buyers have not opposed the program;
- the program has been accepted as budget neutral.

There are two points of vulnerability for the Export Enhancement Program in the near future. The first is in the budgetary arena. Budget neutrality arguments have been abandoned now that CCC stocks are no longer used as bonuses and apparent effects on U.S. prices are small. EEP spending has already been cut about $200 million for fiscal year 1995. The second point is that the GATT in agriculture will require a further reduction of the EEP over time. This makes EEP reform part of a policy package that will make U.S. farmers as well as nonfarmers better off than at present.

References

Salathe, Larry. 1991. Budget neutrality of EEP. U.S. Department of Agriculture, Economic Analysis Staff. Mimeograph. November.

Seitzinger, A. H., and P. L. Paarlberg. 1989. *The Export Enhancement Program.* U.S. Department of Agriculture. Economic Research Service. Agriculture Information Bulletin, no. 575.

U.S. House of Representatives. 1985. Committee on Agriculture. *General Farm Bill of 1985: Hearings before the Committee on Agriculture.* 99th Cong., 1st sess. Pts. 1, 5.

———. 1986. Committee on Agriculture. *Review of the Export Enhancement Program.* 99th Cong., 1st sess. H. Rept. 99-16.

———. 1990. Committee on Agriculture. *Food Security Act of 1985: Report of the Committee on Agriculture to accompany H.R. 2100.* 99th Cong., 1st sess. H. Rept. 101-916. 22 October.

———. 1991. Committee on Agriculture. *Formulation of the 1990 Farm Bill: Hearings before the Committee on Agriculture.* 1–14.

U.S. Senate. 1984. Committee on Agriculture, Nutrition, and Forestry. *Farm policy perspectives: Setting the stage for 1985 agricultural legislation.* 98 Cong., 2nd sess. Committee Print.

———. 1991. Committee on Agriculture, Nutrition, and Forestry. *Preparation for the 1990 Farm Bill.* 101st Cong., 2nd sess. S. Rept. 14 vols.

7 Agricultural Interest Group Bargaining over the North American Free Trade Agreement

David Orden

This paper focuses on the attempts of U.S. agricultural interest groups to influence the outcomes of the North American Free Trade Agreement (NAFTA), which was approved by Congress in November 1993. Agricultural issues have loomed large in world trade discussions since the earlier inception of the Uruguay Round General Agreement on Tariffs and Trade (GATT) negotiations in 1986, and Canada and Mexico are important agricultural trade partners of the United States. For these reasons, the agricultural provisions of NAFTA became an important component of the agreement. Moreover, agricultural interests played a crucial role in the passage of the NAFTA implementing legislation. They were able to win concessions that protect U.S. sugar from Mexican competition and provide transition-period protection to winter fruits and vegetables, and that ensnared the United States in disputes about Canadian exports of wheat and peanut butter. With these concessions, the trade liberalization achieved under NAFTA has resulted in little reform of entrenched domestic agricultural support programs in the United States (or Canada) during the lengthy tariff phaseout periods.

To develop these points, the paper is organized as follows. A brief description of U.S. agricultural trade and support policies is provided, the approaches of the agricultural interest groups toward the negotiations between 1990 and 1992 are examined, and the provisions of the negotiated agreement and estimates of its likely impacts are reviewed. The focus then turns to the side agreements negotiated by the administration of President Bill Clinton after the 1992 elections, the activities of the agricultural interest groups during the con-

David Orden is associate professor of agricultural and applied economics at Virginia Polytechnic Institute and State University.

The author thanks Barbara Craig, Carol Goodloe, and Anne Krueger and other conference participants for helpful comments. He is also indebted to the many participants in the NAFTA debate who shared their insights in interviews and other correspondence.

gressional debate over the implementing legislation, and the final concessions offered to obtain support from agricultural interests. The concluding section addresses some issues raised by the NAFTA outcomes for agriculture.

7.1 Diversity within Agriculture

Agricultural production is only 3 percent of national output but is diffused among many diverse sectors. Grains and oilseeds account for one-fifth of the value of U.S. production, and livestock and poultry products for another one-fifth (International Trade Commission [ITC] 1993). A third group of commodities, important in the NAFTA context, is made up of horticultural products, and a final group are those commodities for which the United States has traditionally imposed import quotas under Section 22 of the Agricultural Adjustment Act of 1935 and its extensions (dairy products, cotton, peanuts, sugar and sugar-containing products).[1]

Grains and oilseeds are generally exported crops, while trade has been less important for livestock and poultry products and most fruits and vegetables (an exception is seasonal winter vegetables, for which imports have a 40 percent market share). Imports of dairy products, cotton, and peanuts have been restricted to less than 2 percent of domestic production, while sugar imports have fallen to 15 percent as domestic output has increased and corn sweeteners have captured a large share of the caloric sweeteners market. Less than 2 percent of dairy products are exported but exports account for more than 40 percent of U.S. cotton and 15 percent of the value of peanut production.[2]

Domestic policy interventions provide high levels of support for some export crops as well as for the Section 22 commodities (see, for example, U.S. Department of Agriculture [USDA] 1994). Support for export crops (including cotton) is provided through supply restrictions, direct payments to producers, floor prices ("loan rates") for government-supported storage, and some export subsidies. Livestock and poultry generally receive few direct support payments and relatively low levels of protection. The support and protection levels have also been relatively low for most fruits and vegetables.

Canada and Mexico are important to U.S. agricultural trade of a number of commodities. Canada produces over one-third of U.S. grain and oilseed imports, including essentially all imported wheat, barley, and soybeans. Canada also produces over 35 percent of U.S. livestock and poultry imports, almost one-third of U.S. imports of peanuts and peanut products, and over one-fourth of imported sugar-containing products. Mexico produces over 90 percent of

---

1. Section 22 authorizes trade restrictions when imports "render ineffective or materially interfere with" domestic supply-control and price-support programs of the U.S. Department of Agriculture.

2. Dairy products are priced above world levels and are exported with subsidies. Peanut exports arise from a two-tier pricing scheme that allows sales at lower world price levels of U.S. peanuts beyond a quantity produced for the domestic market.

imported winter fruits and vegetables and over 10 percent of livestock imports. Canada and Mexico each account for over 15 percent of the value of U.S. livestock and poultry exports and Mexico receives over one-third of U.S. dairy exports.

7.2   Interest Group Approaches to the Negotiations

When the Mexico-U.S. free trade negotiations were announced in June 1990, President Carlos Salinas and President George Bush articulated a broad mandate for reducing bilateral trade barriers and supporting Mexican reforms in agriculture and other sectors. Nevertheless, there was considerable uncertainty about the extent to which agriculture would be included under the mandate for trade liberalization. This uncertainty was created in part by the high levels of protection provided to many commodities in Mexico and the United States. The subsequent entry of Canada into the negotiations added to the uncertainty, since nontariff trade barriers had not been removed in the 1988 Canada-U.S. trade agreement, as described by Miner (1993). Finally, the Uruguay Round GATT negotiations, which had originally been scheduled to conclude in 1990, remained deadlocked on agriculture.

Faced with all this uncertainty, agricultural interest groups took active roles in seeking to shape the provisions of NAFTA. Among the supporters of relatively comprehensive liberalization were the American Farm Bureau Federation, the National Corn Growers Association, numerous other grain, oilseed, and livestock associations, and many processing industries.[3]

Opponents of liberalization included the National Farmers Union, wheat producers (raising concerns about transportation subsidies and the nontransparency of the pricing policies of the monopolistic Canadian Wheat Board), and protected peanut, sugar, and citrus and other winter fruit and vegetable producers. A strong coalition emerged among the Florida sugar and fruit and vegetable interests. They developed a unified position with the Florida Farm Bureau and the Florida Cattlemen's Association (both eventually broke ranks with their national organizations' support for NAFTA), and the state commissioner of agriculture became an active proponent of their concerns. No similar coalition arose among the Section 22 commodities in general because the dairy and cotton sectors (with current or potential export interests in Mexico) remained less opposed than sugar and peanuts to trade liberalization on a bilateral basis.

3. Descriptions of the positions and activities of the various interest groups are based largely on interviews with representatives of twenty-two of the groups most involved in the negotiations and congressional deliberations, as well as with negotiators and others. These interviews were conducted between August and November 1993. Some initial evaluations of NAFTA by representatives of the agricultural interests are also summarized in the reports of the Agricultural Trade Policy Advisory Committee and the Agricultural Technical Advisory Committees.

7.3   Agricultural Provisions of NAFTA

High-level negotiators for Mexico and the United States agreed in February 1992 that all agricultural products would be included in the long-run provisions for trade liberalization. Canada resisted participation in an agreement of such broad scope for agriculture. It agreed only to negotiate extension to Mexico of the limited provisions similar to those of the 1988 Canada-U.S. agreement.

The negotiating parties announced that they had reached a conclusion to their discussions in August. For Mexico and the United States, the agricultural tariff and market access provisions called for the conversion of all nontariff barriers to tariff-rate quotas (TRQs). Under the TRQs, limited quantities of commodities would receive access under low or zero duties, while imports above these quantities would be subject to over-quota tariffs set to provide initial protection equivalent to the previous nontariff measures. The over-quota tariffs were to be phased out over adjustment periods of ten to fifteen years (see U.S. House of Representatives 1993).

The long-run NAFTA provisions for agriculture accomplished the basic objectives with respect to trade barriers of the broader 1987 U.S. "zero-option" GATT proposal for elimination of trade-distorting border measures and support policies. This result led Hufbauer and Schott (1993), for example, to conclude that there was "laudable progress in the liberalization of farm trade barriers."

One cannot be as sanguine about the short-run NAFTA provisions for agriculture. For the commodities protected by import quotas or licenses, market access levels under the initial TRQs were based on 1989 to 1991 trade quantities and were scheduled to increase at only a 3 percent annual compound rate. Over-quota tariffs provided high levels of protection against additional imports in the short and medium run. Corn, dry edible beans, milk powder, and peanuts were considered particularly sensitive commodities and received fifteen-year adjustment periods.

Intense negotiations also focused on complex protective TRQ transition mechanisms for sugar: Mexico agreed to raise its external sugar tariff to the preexisting U.S. over-quota level by the seventh year of the agreement and subsequently gained potentially unlimited access to the U.S. market if it achieved a net production surplus. Special tariff phaseout and TRQ mechanisms were also developed for citrus and other horticultural products.

The influence of various producer groups on the negotiations is evident from the NAFTA transition mechanisms for agricultural trade. Within the framework of long-run liberalization, likely gainers among U.S. producers confront the lengthy adjustment mechanisms included to protect Mexican farmers. Import-competing U.S. commodities are provided with similar adjustment protection. Given these provisions, the end constraint of complete tariff elimination is crucial to the assertion that the negotiated provisions accomplished long-run bilateral trade liberalization for agriculture.

7.4   Estimated Impacts of the Agreement

Among the quantitative studies of the long-run effects of NAFTA on Mexican-U.S. agricultural trade, Grennes and Krissoff (1993) estimated that U.S. agricultural exports to Mexico (primarily grains, oilseeds, and livestock products) would increase by $485 million annually, and agricultural imports from Mexico by $164 million (primarily horticultural commodities and live cattle). The USDA Office of Economics (1993) asserted a more positive view of NAFTA's potentially beneficial impacts. Incorporating projected demand effects resulting from an increase due to NAFTA of 0.5 percent in Mexico's annual economic growth, the USDA concluded that agricultural exports to Mexico were likely to be more than $2.5 billion higher annually with NAFTA by the end of the fifteen-year adjustment period, while imports of agricultural products from Mexico would increase by $500 to $600 million.

7.5   Side Agreements and Implementing Legislation

After the November 1992 election, the Clinton administration followed through on its campaign pledge to negotiate supplemental (side) agreements with respect to the environment, labor, and import surges. The change in administration gave the agricultural commodity groups that had sought limits on NAFTA's trade-liberalizing provisions the opportunity for a second hearing. In particular, the concerns of the sugar producers were acknowledged by the designated United States trade representative, Mickey Kantor. As early as his January 1993 preconfirmation hearings, he pointed out that the side agreement on import surges would "affect agriculture and particularly be protective, we hope, of the sugar industry" (U.S. Senate 1993). Despite such assurances, the side agreement on import surges that was negotiated by the Clinton administration did not achieve the types of changes in the initial NAFTA provisions sought by some agricultural producer groups.

Faced with growing opposition, President Clinton used a September 1993 signing ceremony for the side agreements to launch an intense campaign for passage by Congress of implementing legislation for NAFTA. Agricultural interest groups played an active role in the ensuing congressional debate.

Among supporters of the agreement, an umbrella support organization called Ag for NAFTA was formed and eventually claimed over 140 member organizations. In addition, the American Farm Bureau Federation and many of the specific commodity associations devoted staff and resources to support passage of the implementing legislation. However, the scale of their activities was relatively modest compared to the widespread efforts among interested parties (see, for example, Grayson 1993). Ag for NAFTA had an initial budget of about $10,000 and its final budget for publicity, advertising, and other expenses was less than $100,000.

The commodities receiving Section 22 protection pursued separate approaches to the implementing legislation based on the particular circumstances of each sector. The National Milk Producers Federation adopted a position of support for the agreement during the summer of 1993 and the National Cotton Council of America endorsed NAFTA in October.

Opponents of NAFTA also continued to mobilize around the implementing legislation. The National Farmers Union made defeat of NAFTA one of its top priorities and was a founding member of the opponents' Citizens Trade Campaign. While not formally aligned with third-party presidential aspirant Ross Perot, who was an active NAFTA opponent, representatives of the farmers union believed he had reduced the prospects for the approval of the agreement.

Among specific commodity groups opposing the agreement, wheat producers continued their break with the other export-oriented grains and held out for resolution of the issues of Canadian transportation subsidies and Wheat Board price transparency.[4] In exchange for their support for NAFTA, the wheat producers sought emergency action under Section 22. This would have allowed the Clinton administration to impose immediate quotas or tariffs on grain imported from Canada rather than await the outcome of an investigation and ruling by the ITC.

Peanut and sugar producer groups also remained opposed to the NAFTA provisions. The sugar producers sought two modifications of the initial agreement: inclusion of corn sweeteners in determining the balance of production and consumption affecting Mexican access to the U.S. sugar market and a ceiling on Mexico's access for the full fifteen-year adjustment period. The sugar producers lobbied the USDA and the Office of the U.S. Trade Representative (USTR) and pressed their case through the Senate sweeteners caucus. They viewed the USTR as sympathetic to their interests but nevertheless committed $500,000 to a campaign to "go hell bent to defeat NAFTA" if the agreement was not revised. Their demands, of course, brought into sharp focus the competing interests of different commodity groups within U.S. agriculture, as well as the relative strength of the Mexican and U.S. negotiating positions.

The Florida coalition, working along commodity lines and through the unified position among agricultural groups within the state, also pressed for further accommodations for sugar, citrus, and other winter fruits and vegetables. The Florida agricultural producers, worked closely with the state's congressional delegation of ten Democrats and thirteen Republicans, which throughout the congressional deliberations almost entirely remained on record as opposed to the agreement.

---

4. While the wheat growers were clamoring about Canadian policies, the flow of wheat into the United States resulted as much from the U.S. export subsidies discussed by Bruce Gardner in chapter 6 of this volume.

7.6   End Game Concessions

With the fate of NAFTA uncertain as the November 17 vote in the House of Representatives approached, the agricultural commodity groups were positioned to win various concessions. Unlike organized labor and others committed to the defeat of the agreement, most of the agricultural commodity groups had limited their opposition to specific provisions. Moreover, a relatively large number of congressional votes rested at least in part on satisfying the concerns of the agricultural producers.

The end game exploded into public view in early November. Concessions obtained for agriculture in the last two weeks of the debate are summarized in table 7.1.

7.6.1   Initial Concessions

An initial November 3 letter from the U.S. trade representative to Mexico's secretary of commerce indicated that the United States would seek a mutual agreement on accelerated tariff reductions for wine and brandy (USTR 1993). A second and more significant letter confirmed the USTR's understanding that the two parties had recognized that substitution of corn syrup for sugar could "result in effects not intended by either Party" and therefore agreed that consumption of corn syrup would be included in the determination of Mexico's net production surplus. The letter also indicated that notwithstanding previous provisions, Mexican sugar sales in the United States under NAFTA would be capped at 250,000 metric tons through a fifteen-year adjustment period. In short, Mexico had conceded to the demands of the U.S. sugar producers. Subsequently, the sugar industry indicated that it had withdrawn its opposition to NAFTA, a decision expected to influence at least a dozen votes in the House of Representatives.

A third letter between the U.S. and Mexican negotiators addressed the issues raised by the Florida citrus industry. It specified an explicit price-based tariff snapback for citrus. Under the snapback, the United States would apply the prevailing most-favored-nation (MFN) rate of duty on imports from Mexico in excess of specific quantities if the price of fresh concentrated orange juice dropped below an average based on the preceding five years for five consecutive days.

In addition to this modest change from the original NAFTA text, the citrus producers had bargained for several other concessions: that tariffs on all forms of fresh and processed citrus products would receive the minimum 15 percent cut under the still-pending Uruguay Round GATT, that non-NAFTA citrus juices would be reclassified as perishable commodities under U.S. law (expediting future injury claims by the industry), and that foreign citrus products would not receive additional special status under the Generalized System of Preferences (GSP) or the Caribbean Basin Initiative (CBI). The board of direc-

Table 7.1   Final NAFTA Concessions and Assurances to Agricultural Interests

Wine/brandy	United States to seek mutual agreement to accelerated tariff reductions
Sugar	Consumption of corn sweeteners included in the determination of net production surplus Mexican TRQ capped at 250,000 metric tons for the seventh through fourteenth years of the agreement
Citrus	Most-favored-nation rate of duty on imports from Mexico in excess of 70 million gallons annually through 2002 (90 million gallons during 2003–2007) if the price of fresh concentrated orange juice drops below an average based on the preceding five years for five consecutive days GATT tariff cuts on fresh and processed citrus products limited to 15 percent Non-NAFTA citrus juices to be reclassified as perishable commodities to expedite injury claims Citrus products not to receive additional special status under the GSP or the CBI
Fruits and vegetables	Early warning import-surge mechanism GATT tariff cuts limited to 15 percent on tomatoes, peppers, lettuce, cucumbers, celery, and sweet corn Sensitive products not to receive additional special status under the GSP or the CBI Postponement of decertification of methyl bromide for use as a soil fumigant until 2000 Funding for soil and postharvest fumigant research; completion and funding for U.S. Horticultural Research Station, Fort Pierce, Florida Doubled purchases of fresh tomatoes and new purchases of sweet corn for school lunch programs Trade representative assurance of effective price-based and volume-based tariff snapback provisions for fresh tomatoes and peppers
Wheat	End-use certificates to prevent subsidized reexport of Canadian wheat and barley Bilateral consultations to address transportation subsidies and Canadian Wheat Board pricing practices and an ITC investigation of whether imports interfere with the domestic wheat program within sixty days unless the consultations were successful
Peanuts	Bilateral consultations to address the increase in imports of peanut butter/paste from Canada and an ITC investigation of whether imports interfere with the domestic peanut program within sixty days unless the consultations were successful Secretary of agriculture assurance to work vigorously to limit the volume of imports from Canada
Transshipment	Commissioner of customs assurance of at least ten investigations and 350 positions, including 100 new hires, to enforce rules of origin

tors of Florida Citrus Mutual voted to withdraw their opposition to the agreement on November 10 based on these concessions.

As the anti-NAFTA Florida coalition collapsed, other Florida fruit and vegetable producers also sought accommodations. The administration agreed to a range of concessions that included the use of an early warning import-surge mechanism; limits for certain commodities with respect to GATT, the GSP, and the CBI similar to those offered for citrus; an environmentally controversial postponement of decertification and methyl bromide for use as a soil fumigant;

funding for research on soil treatment and postharvest fumigation; and an agreement to increase purchases of fresh tomatoes and sweet corn for school lunch programs. The board of directors of the Florida Fruit and Vegetable Association withdrew its opposition to NAFTA on November 11.

7.6.2   Final Deals

Passage of the implementing legislation remained uncertain less than a week before the scheduled congressional vote, so the administration and its support-ers could not relax their efforts. Ag for NAFTA brought fifty to sixty leaders of various member organizations to Washington to lobby, but the real action was with the groups that had been or remained opposed to NAFTA.

The wheat producers engaged in tense late-deal bargaining. Their hope for emergency Section 22 quotas or tariffs was scuttled when, by several accounts, the administration determined that they could not influence many votes. On November 15, however, the president agreed to partially accommodate the pro-ducers: he asked that the ITC investigate whether imports from Canada were interfering with U.S. wheat support programs, unless there were successful bilateral negotiations on Canadian policies within sixty days. With this conces-sion, the National Association of Wheat Growers announced, less than thirty-six hours before the House vote, that it would "now work for congressional approval of NAFTA." Five congressmen cited the Wheat Growers' position in support of their final decisions to vote for the implementing legis-lation.

One of these representatives, Representative Glenn English, was also con-cerned about illegal transshipment of peanuts and beef through Mexico. To address the continuing opposition to NAFTA by peanut producers and English's concerns, the president committed the administration to bilateral consultations on imports of peanut butter from Canada and to a second ITC investigation within sixty days if necessary. English was assured by the com-missioner of customs that there would be "at least ten visits to agricultural processing sites in Mexico," and that "350 positions, including 100 newly hired employees," would be assigned to enforce the NAFTA rules of origin.

Final critical decisions were made by the Florida congressional delegation, which held a closed-door meeting on November 16. Although there may al-ready have been several closet votes for NAFTA, an Associated Press poll had counted only five of the twenty-three members of the delegation as supporting or leaning toward supporting the agreement on the previous day. A pivotal se-nior member of the Florida delegation was Representative Tom Lewis, who served on the House Committee on Agriculture. To assure Lewis about his concerns required an additional letter from Mickey Kantor specifying that NAFTA contained "effective price and volume-based snapback provisions to deal with increased imports of fresh tomatoes and peppers." The next day, Lewis and twelve other members of the Florida delegation voted with the administration. The NAFTA implementing legislation passed in the House of Representatives by a 234 to 200 majority.[5]

7.7   Conclusions from the NAFTA Outcomes

In drawing inferences about the political economy of trade protection on the basis of the influence of U.S. agricultural groups on the NAFTA negotiations and implementing legislation, a crucial issue is the extent to which a mechanism was provided for overcoming established protection among agricultural sectors and expanding international markets. The decision to seek long-run liberalization of Mexican-U.S. agricultural trade under NAFTA established a strong objective compared to the limited provisions for agriculture in previous bilateral trade agreements and the significant weakening of the U.S. zero-option proposal in the Uruguay-Round GATT negotiations.[6] The subsequent NAFTA provisions for long-run trade liberalization remained largely intact even with the grueling congressional debate. Many of the concessions offered to U.S. agricultural interest groups weaken the NAFTA transition-period provisions only marginally, and other acknowledged concessions to the interest groups are also relatively minor.

This said, the notion that a trade agreement can serve as an avenue for reform of entrenched domestic U.S. agricultural programs fared poorly under NAFTA. Among the protected U.S. commodities, dairy and cotton came to support the Mexican-U.S. agreement only when strong rules of origin were adopted and the absence of any threat to their domestic markets became apparent. Peanut producers fought hard against the agreement and battled in the end for several concessions to sustain their protection.

More egregious than the dairy, cotton, and peanut provisions, NAFTA initially created a trade-diverting common sugar market between Mexico and the United States. The subsequent concessions to U.S. sugar interests exacerbated

5. In addition to the confirmed concessions, there were rumors in the press that the administration would back away from its intention to raise grazing fees on federal lands and that the proposed increase in the cigarette tax to finance health care reform might be scaled back in exchange for support for NAFTA (*Wall Street Journal* 1993a, 1993b). A possible deal that did not seem to be under consideration (despite the importance of the Florida delegation) would have linked the NAFTA vote to stalled negotiations between the government and sugar and fruit and vegetable producers as they sought an out-of-court settlement on a program to restore the Everglades by reducing agricultural runoff. Whatever the NAFTA deals, health care reform failed to come to a vote in the 103rd Congress and Interior Secretary Bruce Babbitt withdrew his proposal to raise grazing fees in December 1994.

6. The Uruguay Round GATT negotiations were finally concluded in December 1993 and Congress approved legislation implementing the agreement in December 1994. The final agreement for agriculture includes provisions for replacing quantitative restrictions, such as Section 22 quotas, with TRQs and for lowering all tariffs by an average of 36 percent over six years. The agreement also reduces but does not eliminate export subsidies, and caps some domestic support payments to farmers. See Sanderson (1994) and International Agricultural Trade Research Consortium (1994) for further discussion.

the initial distortion by essentially stealing from the Mexican producers some of their potential market opportunity while enhancing the potential demand facing U.S. producers. The concessions obtained gutted the agreement for freer bilateral trade, albeit within a protected common market, for at least the next fifteen years. They also raise the question of whether the agreement to allow unrestricted trade in sugar between Mexico and the United States after fifteen years is ultimately credible.

The differences in the NAFTA outcomes with Mexico compared to Canada are also telling. The U.S. export producer groups were successful with respect to Mexico, which has opened itself to substantial reform of its agricultural policies. Mexican agricultural producer groups that might have benefitted from a stronger agreement in terms of their own export opportunities had only limited countervailing power against the pressure for concessions by import-protected U.S. producers. To insure NAFTA's approval, the U.S. government succeeded in pressing these concessions on the Mexican government.

With Canada the story is different. Throughout the NAFTA process, import-competing Canadian agricultural producers were more effective in defending their established protection than the Mexican producers. Canada's participation in NAFTA was largely ignored in the United States except by a few special interests. But to insure passage of the implementing legislation, the Clinton administration made unilateral promises to several U.S. agricultural commodity groups about their perceived grievances over imports from Canada. Thus one outcome of the process was that it prolonged the disputes between the United States and Canada over wheat, peanut butter, and other products.

Given the focus on Mexico in the public NAFTA debate, the unresolved issues with Canada are a surprising outcome. Subsequent to NAFTA's enactment, the United States offered to settle the agricultural trade disputes with Canada by adopting bilateral free trade in agricultural products. When this offer was declined, the United States reached a bilateral agreement with Canada for temporary trade restrictions on wheat and imposed a global TRQ on peanut butter in its final Uruguay Round GATT tariff schedule. Thus, post-NAFTA agricultural trade between Canada and the United States ends up more laded with barriers than before.

On a somewhat different theme, the bargaining power that agricultural groups held toward the end of the NAFTA debate is striking. The agricultural interest groups were well positioned to bargain for concessions because they sought modifications of specific provisions but did not oppose the entire agreement. The concerns of sugar, the Florida coalition, peanuts, or wheat mattered to the outcome of close to thirty congressional votes.

The question that arises is why other groups didn't do more to put themselves in such a position. The concessions made to agriculture toward the end of the debate were not the only concessions offered by the Clinton administration. One wonders, for example, why the AFL-CIO didn't approach the president with concerns about specific industries and seek additional transition-period protection in these areas in exchange for delivering their support for the agreement. One can imagine a very different coalition having been put together to pass the implementing legislation in such circumstances. Agricultural interests could have found themselves irrelevant to the congressional vote, leaving the sugar and wheat producers to make their case elsewhere. Curiously, one doubts these parties to last-minute concessions were the intended beneficiaries of organized labor's political efforts.

References

Agricultural Policy Advisory Committee. 1992. *Report on the North American Free Trade Agreement.* Washington D.C.: Office of the U.S. Trade Representative.

Agricultural Technical Advisory Committees. 1992. *Reports on the North American Free Trade Agreement.* Washington D.C.: Office of the U.S. Trade Representative.

Grayson, George W. 1993. *The North American Free Trade Agreement.* Headliner Series, no. 299, Foreign Policy Association.

Grennes, Thomas, and Barry Krissoff. 1993. Agricultural trade in a North American free trade agreement. *The World Economy* 16, no. 4:483–502.

Hufbauer, Gary Clyde, and Jeffrey J. Schott. 1993. *NAFTA: An assessment.* Washington, D.C.: Institute for International Economics.

International Agricultural Trade Research Consortium. 1994. *The Uruguay Round Agreement on Agriculture: An evaluation.* Commissioned Paper no. 9. St. Paul, Minn.: University of Minnesota, Department of Agricultural and Applied Economics.

International Trade Commission. 1993. *Potential impact on the U.S. economy and selected industries of the North American Free-Trade Agreement.* Publication no. 2596.

Miner, William M. 1993. Agricultural trade under the klieg lights: Domestic pressures and bilateral frictions. Working Paper. Ottawa, Canada: Carleton University, Center for Trade Policy and Law.

Office of the United States Trade Representative (USTR). 1993. Letters from Administration Officials Prepared in Connection with the NAFTA Debate. Transmitted by Ira S. Shapiro (general counsel, USTR) to Senator Daniel P. Moynihan (chairman, Senate Committee on Finance) on 18 November 1993.

Sanderson, Fred H. 1994. The GATT agreement on agriculture. Working Paper. Washington, D.C.: National Center for Food and Agricultural Policy.

United States Department of Agriculture. 1994. *Estimates of producer subsidy equivalents and consumer subsidy equivalents: Government intervention in agriculture, 1982–1992.* Statistical Bulletin no. 913. Washington D.C.: Economic Research Service, December.

———. Office of Economics. 1993. *Effects of the North American Free Trade Agreement on U.S. agricultural commodities.* Washington D.C.: Economic Research Service, March.

U.S. House of Representatives. 1993. *Message from the president of the United States transmitting North American Free Trade Agreement, supplemental agreements and additional documents.* 103rd Cong., 1st sess. H. Doc. 103-160.

U.S. Senate. 1993. Committee on Finance. *Hearings on the anticipated nomination of*

Mickey Kantor, U.S. Trade Representative Designate. 103rd Cong., 1st sess. Senate Hearings 103-12. 19 January.

Wall Street Journal. 1993a. White House hopes to trade changes in grazing-fee plan for NAFTA support. 10 November.

———. 1993b. Anatomy of a victory: "Deals" and sense of Clinton's commitment clinched NAFTA. 19 November.

8 The Effect of Import Source on the Determinants and Impacts of Antidumping Suit Activity

Robert W. Staiger and Frank A. Wolak

8.1 Introduction

Given the success with which tariff reductions have been negotiated during the postwar period, it is not surprising that the rules which govern the *exceptions* from the negotiated tariff bindings have replaced the tariff bindings themselves as the central focus of international cooperation in trade policy. Nowhere is this change in emphasis more apparent than in the rising friction associated with antidumping law. Accusations that foreign firms are "dumping" products onto the domestic market and the belief that dumping is injurious to the domestic industry are by no means new.[1] Almost eighty years ago, such accusations and beliefs led the United States to adopt its first antidumping legislation, as contained in sections 800–801 of the Revenue Act of 1916. While the original intent of the law was to protect U.S. firms from the "unfair competition" implied by the alleged dumping practices of the highly cartelized and heavily protected German industries of the period (see Viner 1966, 242), antidumping law today seems to elicit a much broader usage.[2]

With the use and abuse of antidumping law now regularly a central concern of both multilateral and bilateral trade negotiations, it is especially important to have as full an understanding as possible of the impact of existing antidump-

Robert W. Staiger is associate professor of economics at The University of Wisconsin-Madison and a research associate of the National Bureau of Economic Research. Frank A. Wolak is associate professor of economics at Stanford University and a research associate of the National Bureau of Economic Research.

1. Dumping is defined as exporting products to the domestic market at export prices "below fair value," that is, either below the prices of comparable products for sale in the domestic market of the exporting country or below costs of production.

2. This broadening usage was in part facilitated by explicit changes in U.S. antidumping law. For example, under the original U.S. law, predatory intent had to be shown to establish a finding of dumping. However, the Revenue Act of 1921 dropped the intent requirement.

ing laws on the free flow of trade, and of the uses to which antidumping law is put in practice. In this regard, several researchers have challenged the view that antidumping law restricts trade only when antidumping duties are actually imposed, arguing that the threat or even the mere possibility of duties can also affect import flows. Here we explore the differences across import sources of the uses and effects of antidumping law, accounting for both direct as well as possible indirect effects on imports and domestic import-competing output.

In an earlier paper (Staiger and Wolak 1994) we studied three possible channels through which these indirect effects might arise, which, we believe, when combined with the direct effects of duties capture most of the trade effects of antidumping law. We referred to these three nonduty effects as the "investigation effect," the "suspension effect," and the "withdrawal effect." The first refers to the trade distortions associated with ongoing antidumping investigations, the second to the effects of "suspension agreements" (under which investigations are suspended in exchange for a promise by foreign firms to stop dumping), and the third to the effects of petitions that are withdrawn prior to a final determination. Our empirical findings, which reflected data on the timing and outcome of every antidumping investigation that covered a manufacturing industry product in the United States between 1980 and 1985, indicated that the investigation and suspension effects are substantial. Specifically, we found that suspension agreements lead to trade restrictions similar in magnitude to what would have been expected if antidumping duties were imposed instead. We found that the effect of a typical antidumping investigation is to reduce imports during the period of investigation by roughly half the reduction that could be expected if antidumping duties had been imposed from the beginning of the investigation. We found little evidence to support a significant withdrawal effect.

Our focus on the broader trade effects of antidumping law also allowed us to consider the possibility that different firms might file antidumping petitions for different reasons. In particular, we found evidence of two distinct filing strategies that appeared to coexist in the data, and we referred to firms as "outcome filers" or "process filers," depending on which strategy they appeared to be using. Outcome filers are firms that file antidumping petitions in anticipation of obtaining a finding of dumping and the relief that comes with it (either antidumping duties or a settlement agreement). Process filers are firms that file antidumping petitions not to obtain a dumping finding, but rather to obtain the effects that arise solely from the investigation process itself. Our estimates suggested that while outcome filers are by far the dominant users of antidumping law, process filing was the likely strategy used by between 3 and 4 percent of the industries in our sample.

In the present paper we continue this line of research by looking for evidence of differences in the use and impacts of U.S. antidumping law as it is applied to imports from different trading partners. As we discuss in section 8.2, whether an antidumping petition is initiated for process- or outcome-filing reasons should depend not only on the characteristics of the domestic industry but also on the characteristics of the exporting country or countries against which the petition is filed. In our earlier work we allowed for the possibility that filing strategies might differ across U.S. industries, but we required firms in a given industry to pursue a common filing strategy against foreign imports, regardless of the country of origin. In this paper we allow the filing strategies of firms to be different for different import sources, but we impose the restriction that firms in all U.S. industries pursue the same overall filing strategy. Thus we consider the possibility that U.S. firms may be outcome filers against imports from some countries and process filers against others.

Using this method of analysis we are able to quantify significant differences in filing strategies used by U.S. industries against five sets of trading partner countries. We also are able to quantify the extent of import and domestic output distortions due to the various stages of the suit resolution process for each of these five sets of trading partners. Finally, we are able to distinguish between regions exporting to the United States that are primarily targets of process filings by U.S. industries, as well as those regions that are primarily targets of outcome filings by U.S. industries.

The rest of the paper proceeds as follows. Section 8.2 describes our motivation for including investigation, suspension, and withdrawal effects with the duty effects when quantifying the impact of antidumping law on imports and domestic output. It then describes the different investigation effects expected under outcome- and process-filing strategies. We also discuss in this section why some countries are more likely than others to be the target of process filing by U.S. firms. Section 8.3 then describes our empirical findings. Section 8.4 concludes.

8.2   U.S. Antidumping Law

We begin by making several observations concerning the practice of antidumping law in the United States which may be helpful to keep in mind. First, there are two findings necessary for a determination of dumping: (1) sales of imports at less than fair value (LTFV), and (2) material injury to the domestic industry due to these imports. One government agency is assigned to each of these determinations—the International Trade Commission (ITC) determines injury to the domestic industry and the Commerce Department's International Trade Administration (ITA) makes the LTFV determination. A second point to bear in mind is that for each of these decisions there is a preliminary and final decision made by each agency. The statutory time allotted for the entire investigation ranges from ten months to fourteen months under special circumstances. Finally, except in "critical circumstances" (a condition described more fully below but in practice rarely met), a final determination of dumping will bring the retroactive imposition of antidumping duties on all imports of the relevant products which entered the United States on or after the date of the preliminary LTFV finding, provided that the preliminary LTFV finding was affirmative (as it was for 93 percent of the products whose investigations made it to this stage of the investigation process between 1980 and 1985). With these general points in mind we now turn to a discussion of the various potential trade distorting effects of antidumping law.

8.2.1   The Trade Effects of Antidumping Law

A simple view of the trade effects of antidumping law would hold that trade flows are affected by antidumping law only when a petition is filed, dumping is found, and antidumping duties are imposed. However, there are a number of reasons to believe that this simple view is inadequate and that many of the effects of antidumping law are indirect and subtle. We now describe three non-duty effects which, we believe, when combined with the effects of duties, capture a major component of the possible trade effects of antidumping law.

The Investigation Effect

First, it is often claimed (see, for example, Dale 1980, 85–86 and U.S. Congress 1978, 12, 278) that imports are restricted during the period in which an antidumping investigation is taking place. There are two broad hypotheses concerning the reasons for and nature of this investigation effect. We refer to these two hypotheses as the "outcome-filer" hypothesis and the "process-filer" hypothesis. According to the outcome-filer hypothesis, the investigation effect reflects actions taken by domestic importers and/or foreign exporters in anticipation of the duties that would be imposed in the event of a final affirmative dumping determination and that would be assessed retroactively back to the date of an affirmative preliminary LTFV determination. That is, as noted above, an affirmative preliminary LTFV determination carries with it the liability of duty assessment for all imports entering thereafter if a final affirmative dumping determination is subsequently made. Consequently, a preliminary finding of LTFV sales would be expected under this hypothesis to lead to a sharp drop in imports, with these trade-restricting effects lasting for the remainder of the investigation period, as long as the petition was perceived as having a reasonable chance of ending in a final dumping determination.

In addition to a drop in imports coming with an affirmative preliminary LTFV determination, the outcome-filer hypothesis carries with it two additional implications. First, in light of the possibility of an affirmative preliminary LTFV determination and a subsequent falloff in import flows, imports might, if anything, be expected to rise somewhat during the first months of the investigation in anticipation of this effect. In fact, evidently anticipating this possibility, U.S. law provides for an assessment of "critical circumstances" under which duties can be imposed retroactively back to the date of filing if the filing of a petition brings with it a significant import surge. For this reason, we would expect any import increase associated with the early stages of an investigation under the outcome-filer hypothesis to be small. Second, under the outcome-filer hypothesis, any petitions filed without regard to measures important for the final dumping determination would be unlikely to exhibit strong investigation effects, since this hypothesis presumes a significant probability of a final dumping determination and consequent duty imposition. It is for this reason that we refer to this hypothesis as the outcome-filer hypothesis: the strength of the investigation effect under this hypothesis reflects the fear of retroactive duty imposition in the event of an affirmative final determination at the end of the investigation process, and therefore ought to reflect the likelihood that the final outcome will be a finding of dumping.

It is also possible that there are investigation effects that do *not* reflect a significant probability of retroactive duty imposition at the end of the investigation process, but reflect the effects of the investigation process itself. This embodies the process-filer hypothesis. In an earlier paper (Staiger and Wolak 1991) we presented a model in which domestic firms make strategic use of the ongoing antidumping investigation of the pricing and sales practices of foreign firms to prevent the occurrence of price wars which might otherwise be triggered by periods of slack demand and low capacity utilization. Our theory suggests that domestic firms may value the competition-dampening effects of an ongoing antidumping investigation for its own sake, and may file such petitions when capacity utilization is low with no expectation that they would actually result in duties or other remedies. In Staiger and Wolak (1994) we referred to such filers as process filers, and noted that (1) the act of filing ought to have an immediate trade-dampening effect which lasts for the duration of the investigation, distinguishing the investigation effects under process filers from those under outcome filers; and that (2) process filers ought to file antidumping petitions on the basis of low capacity utilization and little else, and in particular should not be concerned with measures important for the final determination of dumping, thus distinguishing the filing behavior under process filers from that of outcome filers.

The Suspension Effect

Turning to the suspension effect, a second way in which antidumping law may restrict trade through nonduty channels is through the effects of so-called suspension agreements, under which antidumping investigations are suspended by the Commerce Department in exchange for an explicit agreement by foreign firms named in the antidumping petition to eliminate sales in the U.S. market at less than "fair value." Since the intent of a suspension agreement is to provide a nonduty alternative by which previous dumping activities can be halted, it would be surprising if there were not a suspension effect in the data. A prominent example involving such a suspension agreement (though not falling in our sample period) was the 1986 U.S.-Japan Semiconductor Trade Agreement.

The Withdrawal Effect

Finally, a third way in which antidumping law may restrict trade through nonduty channels concerns the withdrawal effect.[3] That is, the imposition of antidumping duties or the negotiation of a suspension agreement need not be the only outcomes of an antidumping petition for which postinvestigation relief from imports is secured. In this regard, Prusa (1992) has argued that petitions which are withdrawn by the domestic industry before a final determination can have as restrictive an impact on subsequent trade flows as would be the case if a final determination of dumping had been made and duties imposed. Essentially, Prusa argues that domestic firms can use the threat of antidumping duties, together with the protection from domestic antitrust laws afforded when an antidumping proceeding is in progress, to bargain with foreign firms over domestic market share, and that the antidumping petition is withdrawn by the domestic industry if and when an acceptable bargain is struck.[4]

8.2.2   The Targets of Process Filers

The logic of our process-filer strategy is that domestic firms use the antidumping investigation process to reduce the temptation of foreign firms to cut prices during periods of low capacity utilization. For this strategy to be sensible for domestic firms to pursue over our sample period, several conditions must be met in the country (countries) against which this filing strategy is being used. First, the firms exporting from each country named in the antidumping petition should comprise a significant share of the relevant U.S. market, since otherwise the threat posed by these firms to the profitability of U.S. firms in the event of a breakdown in price discipline is likely to be small. Second, the U.S. market share captured by the firms exporting from these countries should be relatively stable over the sample period, since otherwise the premise of an orderly pricing arrangement, whose breakdown during periods of falling capacity utilization can be avoided through the competition-dampening effects of antidumping investigations, would be in doubt. Third, exporters from these countries should be relatively dependent on the U.S. market for their sales, since otherwise demand shifts in the U.S. market which lead to falling capacity utilization of U.S. firms might not lead to a significant fall in capacity utilization rates for the foreign exporters (and therefore would not

---

3. In addition, a number of papers (e.g., Anderson 1992, Staiger and Wolak 1992, and Prusa 1988) have suggested that the mere existence of antidumping law can have trade effects even in periods when no petition is filed.

4. Agreements between foreign firms and domestic petitioners are permitted under the Noerr-Pennington doctrine, which provides exemption from prosecution under U.S. antitrust law. Direct conversations between domestic and foreign firms concerning prices or quantities would not be protected, so settlements are typically negotiated through the Commerce Department (Gary Horlick, personal communication, 1989). See Prusa (1992) for a detailed analysis of this exemption and its implications for the effects of antidumping law.

give rise to a significant temptation on the part of foreign exporters to cut prices in the U.S. market).

With these three criteria in mind, the countries likely to be targets of process filings in the United States during our 1980–85 sample period are those whose export production over this period is predominantly destined for the U.S. market and accounts for a relatively large and stable U.S. market share. On this basis, we expect that Canada and Mexico would be the most likely targets of process filings from U.S. firms during our sample period.

8.3   The Uses and Impacts of Antidumping Law

Analyzing the filing behavior against imports from Canada and Mexico as well as against imports from four other regional groupings, we find evidence in the filing behavior and in the nature of the trade impacts which accompany filing to suggest that Canada and Mexico were indeed the most likely targets of antidumping petitions filed under the process-filing strategy during our sample period. That is, the pattern of filing by U.S. firms against imports from Canada and Mexico is primarily predicted by low levels of capacity utilization, and the impact of the investigation on trade flows is to reduce the rate of imports during the entire period of investigation. The regions against which the filing strategy of U.S. firms and the nature of the associated trade impacts seem most consistent with our outcome-filing view of antidumping suit activity are Western Europe and the region composed of Japan and the newly industrialized countries (NICs) of East Asia. That is, the pattern of filing by U.S. firms against imports from these regions is predicted by a broader set of variables which enter into the final determination of dumping, and the impact of the investigation on trade flows is to reduce the rate of imports only at the point of a preliminary LTFV determination.

As for the differing effects of investigation outcomes on postinvestigation imports and domestic output, our parameter estimates imply that the imposition of antidumping duties against any region strongly reduces imports of the products involved, while the response of domestic import-competing output is positive but less precisely estimated. Petitions against a region which are subsequently withdrawn appear to have no lasting effects on imports or domestic output, confirming our earlier findings (Staiger and Wolak 1994). Finally, the paucity of suspension agreements in our sample makes it difficult to assess regional differences in their impacts on postinvestigation imports and domestic output (the Japan-NICs region, for example, did not negotiate any suspension agreements with the United States during our sample period).

We can use our estimates to provide a rough idea of the magnitudes of all the trade-distorting effects, by region and by type of effect, that are associated with the use of antidumping law during our sample period. For our sample of industries and for the six years of available data, the total amount of U.S. import reductions from all investigation effects against Western Europe amounts of approximately -0.05 percent of total (multilateral) U.S. imports over the sample period, while the total distortions attributable to postinvestigation effects against Western Europe is -1.14 percent of total imports over the sample period. For Japan and the NICs, the distortions to U.S. imports from investigation and postinvestigation effects from petitions against this region amounts to 0.87 percent and -2.31 percent, respectively, of total U.S. imports.[5] For both these regions, the major import distortions associated with the use of antidumping law are attributable to postinvestigation effects. For Mexico and Canada, on the other hand, the relative importance of investigation and postinvestigation effects is reversed: the distortions to U.S. imports associated with investigation and postinvestigation effects of petitions against Mexico and Canada are -0.84 percent and -0.25 percent, respectively, of total U.S. imports. This conforms to our findings that U.S. firms appear to be outcome filers against Europe and Japan and the NICs, and hence the main import restrictions come with the explicit remedies provided by the law (duties or suspension agreements), while U.S. firms appear to be process filers against Mexico and Canada, and hence the main import restrictions come from the investigation effects.

A final implication of our process-filer/outcome-filer distinction is that the frequency with which outcome filers ought to secure duties should be substantially higher than for process filers. To investigate this hypothesis we computed the per-suit level of duty activity against Mexico and Canada, the region against which U.S. firms appear to be process filers. We then repeated this same calculation for Europe and Japan and the NICs, treating this as the aggregate region against which U.S. firms appear to be outcome filers. Dividing the "outcome filer ratio" by the "process filer ratio" yields 3.73, suggesting that in our sample, a product-level antidumping petition is 3.73 times more likely to end in duties when it is filed against firms in Europe, Japan, or the NICs than when it is filed against firms from Canada or Mexico. This result is consistent with the view that suits against Canada and Mexico are filed less for the eventual protection provided by duties than are suits against Europe and Japan and the NICs.

8.4 Conclusion

Our cross-country analysis of the determinants and impacts of antidumping suits has revealed a substantial amount of heterogeneity among the different trading regions. Against Western Europe and Japan and the NICs, the use of antidumping law appears to be consistent with the view that firms file in expectation of obtaining relief via antidumping duties or suspension agreements—

5. The positive boost to U.S. imports associated with investigation effects of petitions against Japan and the NICs reflects the fact that the effect of filing on imports is positive and relatively large and that the effect of an affirmative preliminary LTFV determination, while negative, does not persist long enough to reverse this cumulative positive effect.

outcome filers in our nomenclature. This is suggested by the pattern of filing against these regions, which appears to reflect a concern for meeting the injury requirements necessary to secure a finding of dumping, as well as by the import and domestic output responses to filing and the various phases of the suit resolution process. But we have also argued that a distinctive filing strategy against Canada and Mexico would be expected on a priori grounds, and in particular that Canada and Mexico are the most likely targets of process filing by U.S. firms during our sample period because their export production is predominantly destined for the U.S. market and accounts for a relatively high and stable U.S. market share. We find evidence in the use of antidumping law against Mexico and Canada which is consistent with our process-filer logic, where firms file primarily to obtain the protection afforded during the investigation process itself. This is supported by the pattern of filing against these countries, which appears to be driven primarily by the level of capacity utilization but is unrelated to other observable measures of injury, as well as by the import and domestic output responses to filing and the various phases of the suit resolution process.

References

Anderson, James E. 1992. Domino dumping, I: Competitive exporters. *American Economic Review* 82 (March): 65–83.
Dale, Richard. 1980. *Anti-dumping law in a liberal trade order.* New York: St. Martin's Press.
International Monetary Fund. 1987. *Direction of trade statistics yearbook.* Washington, D.C.: International Monetary Fund.
Prusa, Thomas J. 1988. Pricing behavior without settlements. In International trade policies, incentives, and firm behavior. Ph.D. diss., Stanford University.
———. 1992. Why are so many antidumping petitions withdrawn? *Journal of International Economics,* August, 1–20.
Staiger, Robert W., and Frank A. Wolak. 1991. Strategic use of antidumping law to enforce tacit international collusion. Stanford University. Manuscript, March.
———. 1992. The effect of antidumping law in the presence of foreign monopoly. *Journal of International Economics,* May, 265–87.
———. 1994. Measuring industry specific protection: Antidumping in the United States. *Brookings Papers on Economic Activity: Microeconomics,* June.
———. 1996. Differences in the uses and effects of antidumping law across import sources. In *The political economy of American trade policy,* ed. Anne O. Krueger. Chicago: University of Chicago Press, forthcoming.
U.S. Congress. 1978. House Committee on Ways and Means. Subcommittee on Trade. *Administration's comprehensive program for the steel industry: Hearing before the Committee on Ways and Means.* 95th Cong. 2nd sess. 25 and 26 January.
Viner, Jacob. 1966. *Dumping: A problem in international trade.* New York: Augustus M. Kelley Publishers.

9   Implications of the Results of Individual Studies

Anne O. Krueger

The experience with protectionist pressures and protection in the seven industries reported on here, along with the cross-section evidence gleaned from International Trade Administration–International Trade Commission (ITA-ITC) cases, suggest a number of hypotheses.

For economists, some of the important lessons emerge from conclusions regarding the determinants of protection. The Staiger-Wolak findings, the analysis of decisions regarding lumber, the determinants of influence in affecting NAFTA, and, indeed, all the other studies point strongly to the influence of political strength (generally unrelated to considerations of static or dynamic efficiency and even to income distribution arguments often heard) as a major determinant of protection. This appears to be so even for the administered protection processes, which in theory are governed by legal considerations set out in law.[1]

From the perspective of politicians and policymakers, this conclusion will hardly appear surprising. From the viewpoint of the public interest, however, it raises significant questions as to the feasibility of devising institutions or mechanisms which can differentiate between those seeking protection out of narrow self-interest and those cases in which industrial protection might be warranted because of the sorts of considerations to which the "new trade theory" points. For economists concerned with framing policy, therefore, questions as to the capacity of the political process to be constrained in ways which enable trade policy to respond to broader interests must be addressed.

Anne O. Krueger is professor of economics at Stanford University and a research associate of the National Bureau of Economic Research.

1. But the law itself permits the International Trade Commission only to consider factors *within the industry* in determining outcomes: from the viewpoint of economic theory, evaluation should surely take into account the effects on the American economy as a whole, and not simply on the industry receiving protection.

In the volume arising out of the project, these and related issues are dealt with at much greater length. Here the focus is on the findings from the individual studies relevant for the policy-making community regarding current trade policy formulation and practice.

A starting point must be a brief survey of the salient findings from the individual studies. Thereafter, I address the key questions they raise for policy formulation and execution.

9.1   Findings from Individual Studies

9.1.1   Automobiles

From a policy perspective, perhaps the key findings arising from the auto study center on the effects of protection on the industry. It seems clear that voluntary export restraints (VERs) on Japanese automobiles did not achieve the results the automakers apparently hoped for: on one hand, the VER was largely offset initially by a decline in demand (as a result of the recession), thus making the VER ineffective, and later it resulted in higher profits for Japanese companies (thus strengthening their competitive position) as well as increased imports from other countries. Nelson's analysis convincingly demonstrates that the turnaround for U.S. automakers was a result of competition, and not of protection per se.

It should also be noted that VERs were adopted when administration officials began to be concerned that congressional pressures would otherwise result in an even more protectionist outcome: there were bills pending in Congress that would have mandated even more restrictive measures governing auto imports than the VERs on Japanese automobiles. Thus the fact that VERs were employed does not at all prove that the administration was in the forefront of those seeking more protection: the administration moved to forestall congressional action.

9.1.2   Steel

Like automobiles, steel appears to have been experiencing economic difficulties in large part because the earlier high degree of industry concentration and world preeminence had left it very comfortable, unaccustomed to responding to competitive challenges from other sources of supply.

There are several other aspects of the experience with steel that are of interest. First, it is not evident whether the various protectionist measures imposed on steel imports did in fact help the domestic industry. Second, a new technology—the emergence of minimills—resulted in greatly reduced cohesion within the industry in seeking protection. Moreover, some steel users became active opponents of steel protection. This is a clearcut case where the "indirect" effects of protection are important, and the only instance in the seven studies where using industries became at all significant as opponents of protection. Third, when the steel industry was still cohesive in seeking protection, it used the administered trade processes, antidumping and countervailing duties, as an instrument to induce the executive branch to take action. Finally, the effectiveness of a well-organized and cohesive industry effort (for or in the case of steel users, against) in lobbying for a desired outcome was certainly important in the steel industry.

9.1.3 Semiconductors

The semiconductor industry represents another instance where administered trade processes were used to induce the American and Japanese governments to agree upon a VER rather than permit the administered protection process to reach its conclusion. It also represents another instance in which a number of questions may be raised as to whether the protection that resulted helped the U.S. industry: profits were increased for existing Japanese firms, thus enabling them to invest in the next generation of chips that much sooner; third-party effects were important as Korean firms were attracted into the industry by the higher world prices; and Japanese firms located plants within the United States to avoid U.S. protection.

Although the opposition of downstream users of semiconductors proved important in limiting the extent of protection, the semiconductor negotiations raise significant questions as to the extent to which U.S. trade policy can be driven by the interests of one or a few firms. As Douglas Irwin notes, at one point, the position of the U.S. Trade Representative (USTR) was that of one firm (Micron), and the industry held virtual veto power over negotiated agreements.

9.1.4 Textiles and Apparel

The very fact that the textiles and apparel industry has been protected since the mid-1950s raises questions about the efficacy of protection as an instrument to achieve the goals desired by the industry. Employment was declining before the industry received protection; when it did receive protection, new plants opened in the South but plants in New England closed. One analysis suggests that protection accelerated the rate at which the industry relocated to the South (Isard 1973).

The evolution of the protection of the industry also attests to the extent to which an instrument, once in place, tends to become more complex over time as more and more groups attempt to seize it for their own purposes. Finally, J. Michael Finger and Ann Harrison point to the coherence of the industry's organization and lobbying activities: they attribute some of the restrictiveness of the Multi-Fibre Arrangement (MFA), as well as its perpetuation, to that effectiveness.

9.1.5   Lumber

As Joseph Kalt demonstrates, Canadian policy toward lumber results in intramarginal transfers, but economic analysis demonstrates fairly clearly that it does not affect exports to the United States. Despite that, the U.S. industry has been able to appeal to the administered protection process to achieve protection which, in that instance, Kalt judges to be of substantial benefit to the industry by raising the United States' price of lumber.

In evaluating the arguments that are effective in achieving a ruling favorable to the industry seeking protection, Kalt finds that the political influence of the participants is a significant factor in determining the outcome: that is, when the potential gains from winning are significant and the group seeking protection is politically influential, protection is more likely to follow from the process.

9.1.6   Wheat

The wheat Export Enhancement Program (EEP) subsidizes wheat exports. The economic benefits to wheat growers are small relative to the cost of the subsidies, and the question is why, in the absence of a strong rationale, these subsidies have persisted since their initial introduction.

Bruce Gardner points to the unity between the farmers and agribusiness as a key factor in achieving continuing support for the EEP. Notably, also, domestic wheat users have not opposed the program. The fact that EEP supporters are well organized and effective in their political representation has been important. It is also significant that the program was found to be budget-neutral (because of the existence of large government stocks), which enabled Congress to support the program without budgetary consequences.

9.1.7   Agriculture in NAFTA

Whereas the EEP affects only one group of farmers, negotiations over NAFTA potentially affected many groups. Analysis of the positions of various farm groups and the determinants of the degree to which groups received benefits under NAFTA is therefore informative as to the relative strength of different groups.

Perhaps the most significant result to emerge from an analysis of the factors influencing the outcome for different agricultural commodities under NAFTA is the starting point for David Orden's analysis: it was predetermined that, at the end of a (fairly long) transition period, all agricultural protection between the United States and Mexico would be removed. That decision, in an important way, set the agenda and determined the context in which various agricultural groups could attempt to influence the outcome: they could slow down the process but not stop it.

A second significant result of the analysis of the determinants of NAFTA is the extent to which those who remained "moderate" until the final moments before the NAFTA accord reached Congress were able to extract relatively large gains (in terms of their narrowly defined self-interest) in return for their support. Sugar producers, for example, did well because of their willingness to compromise.

9.2   Questions for Policymakers

From the perspective of policy analysis, these findings raise several key issues. First is the extent to which protection achieves the results its supporters hope for, even within their own industries. Second is the extent to which current U.S. trade law and implementation appropriately reflect U.S. interests and, related to that, the questions that arise regarding the frequent failure of user groups to be represented when policy is formulated. Third, the importance of industry unanimity and the absence of opposition from user groups as an important determinant of protection raises a number of questions. While "political strength" matters greatly to an industry's ability to receive protection, that strength can rest on factors other than industry size or even the importance to the industry of receiving protection. Political strength can result from being strategically positioned in the middle of an issue—those in such a position may not be the ones with the most to gain or lose. Fourth, direct winners and losers from protection are not all equal in their attempts to influence the process. In that sense, good lobbying, effective organization, and the means of seeking political representation all matter. Finally, from several of the studies it emerges that once the battle for protection is initially won, the barrier to continued protection is greatly reduced.

9.2.1   Does Protection Help the Protected Industry?

There has been protection for textiles and apparel since the mid-1950s. The first such measure was termed the "Short-Term." Despite that, the industry has chronically complained that protection is "inadequate" and does not "help enough." Despite increasing restrictiveness, especially in the late 1980s, protests from the industry have not diminished.

Protection for automobiles (also in the form of voluntary export restraints) does not appear to have reversed the fortunes of the U.S. automobile industry: Douglas Nelson concludes that competition was the important stimulant.[2] The same questions can be raised about the semiconductor agreement (although industry representatives appear to believe that they were assisted by the semiconductor agreement). For steel, a technological change—the emergence of the minimills—seems to have been important in affecting the industry: it is questionable how much the old integrated mills benefited from VERs on steel

2. See Scherer (1992). Scherer notes that firms in general react more "passively" to foreign competition when trade barriers are in place and, because of that, have less satisfactory performance.

imports. Even in the case of wheat, Gardner believes that the Export Enhancement Program arguably did little for wheat growers, and certainly did less than their enthusiastic support for the program suggests they believed it would.

Among the protected industries studied in the NBER project, then, there is only one instance in which the author believes that U.S. producers unequivocally benefited: lumber. In all the others, it cannot be persuasively argued that the protection accorded an industry was important in turning its fortunes around.[3] This does raise important questions about the efficacy of protectionist trade policies, even in assisting the industries that seek protection. To the extent that trade barriers give producers false assurances, they may indeed be counterproductive from the industry's perspective in the long run.

9.2.2   Does Current Trade Law Reflect U.S. Interests?

There are powerful grounds for arguing that the United States is so important in the international economy that its actions significantly affect the actions undertaken by its trading partners. Certainly other countries have recently been adopting "unfair trading" laws covering countervailing duties and antidumping that are patterned after U.S. law.[4]

The United States clearly has a systemic interest in an open international trading system that by far outweighs the benefits (if any) that can be achieved from individual affirmative findings in administered protection cases, the imposition of VERs, and other protective measures. Even if protection through any of these channels could be shown unequivocally to benefit the American economy, questions could still be raised about the total effect when repercussions on foreign countries are taken into account.

Quite aside from that overarching concern, however, there are grounds for concern about the impact of protection that are not recognized in political debates about trade policy and in the criteria used in U.S. trade law for determining whether protection is warranted. A first and obvious omission, long noted by economists, is that the interests of final consumers are not represented. In political debates, this is no doubt a reflection of the organization costs among large numbers of individuals, each of whom has a small amount to gain if a particular product's price is lower.

However, even more surprising is the fact that under U.S. trade law, the ITC is not empowered to take consumer interests into account in its findings with respect to administered protection. Moreover, the ITC is not even permitted to

3. NAFTA is only now going into effect, and therefore the question of the benefits to different agricultural groups cannot be addressed.

4. There are a number of criticisms that can be made of U.S. trade laws, in addition to those made here. Chief among them are: (1) the law is administered in ways which provide protection even during the period when litigation is proceeding—the Staiger-Wolak finding; (2) the procedures for construction of costs, and other aspects of administrative procedures, can result in findings of "selling below cost" even when the foreign firm is not doing so; and (3) there are circumstances in which foreign firms can be found guilty of practices which, if adopted by an American firm, would be legal. See the essays in Boltuck and Litan (1991).

consider the impact of protection on *other American industries,* including users of the product.[5] Thus, even if economists could convincingly show that the effect of protection on other American industries was quantitatively more harmful (because, for example, of a loss of competitiveness vis-à-vis imports) than the benefits[6] to the prospectively protected industry, that would not constitute sufficient evidence to reject protection.

It should be noted that the failure to consider the "general equilibrium" consequences of protection is a characteristic of political debates on protection as well. Debates over protection for steel and machine tools come to mind as particularly telling examples where the products are purchased primarily by other producers and increased prices inevitably raise their cost structure. But the experience with semiconductors—where producers of personal computers discovered that they would be at a significant disadvantage vis-à-vis their foreign competitors—also vividly illustrates the point.

Even when users are not concentrated in a few industries, the effects on other industries of raising costs can be significant. Yet in all these instances, the political process treats protection to the industry seeking it as something that can be accomplished without harming other sectors of the American economy. Not only is protection itself an economic act of discriminating against the many in favor of the few, but the political and administrative criteria used for awarding protection are biased in that direction. While it might be the case that, for example, society deems that the benefits of protection to apparel exceed the costs, a procedure (or rules of political discourse) which at least permitted these costs to be taken into account would be far preferable to present practices.

9.2.3 There Will Be Protection when the Industry Is Unanimous

Perhaps the most intriguing finding arising from the studies and from discussions with policymakers is the reluctance of using industries to oppose protection, and the general belief that protection will be granted when the industry is unanimous in supporting it.[7]

The most effective defense against protection would appear to be a division within the industry. The most vivid example of this among the NBER cases is steel, where prospects for protection diminished substantially after the owners of minimills opposed it. For semiconductors as well, industry unanimity was not achieved prior to the mid-1980s: until that time, the industry's efforts to

---

5. There is the question, of course, as to why users do not oppose the imposition of protection on their inputs. As seen in Moore's analysis of steel, they can so oppose (if the protection sought is through VERs, but not if it is through the ITC), but it seems to require a fairly major stake in the outcome to induce the necessary organization.

6. It is assumed here that the benefits of protection to the protected industry are positive. As indicated above, however, even this assumption may be suspect.

7. This regularity was noted by several of the "witnesses" when participants in the projects met with policymakers in Washington, D.C., in July 1993. The same point has been made by Milner (1988).

obtain protection had failed. Evidence from other sources and all analysts' accounts point to the same conclusion.

This raises a number of interesting, and unanswered, questions. Why, for example, did the auto industry—a major steel user and itself in difficulty—not oppose steel VERs in the early 1980s? Why did it take until the late 1980s for producers of agricultural machinery to finally oppose continued protection for steel? And, to cite another example, why do apparel makers side *with* textile manufacturers in seeking protection when, as using industries, their interests in textile protection would appear to diverge?[8]

When policymakers were queried in this regard at the project meeting in Washington, responses generally focused upon a "gentleman's agreement," or understanding, that each industry would not protest others' protection, but rather seek its own (implicitly, unopposed). If such is the case, questions arise as to how such tacit understandings came about. If there are not such implicit understandings, the puzzle remains as to why opposition is not more frequently voiced.

9.2.4   Good Lobbying and Organization Do Matter

Short-term economic interests generally determine the side on which various interest groups fall in pressuring for or against protection. However, some groups are better organized, or more readily organized, than others. The correlation between the magnitude of economic interests and the effectiveness of organized lobbying efforts does not appear strong. Some groups that might benefit from protection (or its removal) do not appear well organized, while others are extremely effective.

J. Michael Finger and Ann Harrison point to the well-organized efforts of the textile and apparel groups as a key factor in their achieving as much protection as they in fact receive. Michael Moore's discussion shows the importance of effective organization and lobbying in seeking and maintaining protection.[9]

Protection for the semiconductor industry appears to have been another instance in which a well-organized industry group was crucial to the achievement of protection. Once there was opposition from users (the personal computer assemblers, who had to compete with foreign assemblers), the degree to which the industry could seek to achieve protection diminished.

In this regard, however, perhaps the most interesting and telling cases among the studies are those concerning agriculture: maneuvering regarding the timetable for reduced protection to agriculture under Mexican entry into NAFTA

8. Here, of course, a possible answer might be that the two industries together form a more effective lobby that can achieve more than either could separately, and that the joint gains exceed the potential if each goes it alone.

9. The needed degree of effectiveness is clearly greater for achieving initial protection than for perpetuating it. Even when protection is perpetuated, however, it can be restrictive to varying degrees. A more effective lobby will, presumably, achieve greater restrictiveness than a less effective one.

was heavily influenced by the pressures that different producer groups were able to bring to bear. Likewise, the wheat growers were able to organize to achieve the Export Enhancement Program in ways that other farm groups apparently were not.

9.2.5   Past Protection Matters

The evidence from these studies and elsewhere strongly suggests that the existence of a protectionist instrument—VER, EEP, sugar quota, or whatever—in the past strongly increases the ease with which protection may be obtained today. Stated otherwise, the expected level of protection in the future is higher, for the same industry characteristics, (1) if the industry received protection in the past and (2) the higher the level of protection was in the past.

Clearly, each round of MFA negotiations started with the preceeding level as a base: much of the industry's lobbying efforts were directed to achieving heightened protection. Likewise, Gardner points to the ease with which the wheat growers were enabled to achieve a renewal of the EEP, contrasted with the initial barrier to obtaining it. A semiconductor agreement with Japan in 1991 was far easier to obtain because there had been one in 1986. The history of protection for steel in the 1970s made it easier for the industry to persuade the U.S. administration to negotiate again.

9.3   Interrelationships

Each of these key findings, which are spelled out in considerably greater detail in the conference volume, has implications for policymakers. They are, however, interrelated and when taken in the aggregate suggest that current practices regarding protection may be widely at variance with considerations of the public good or economic efficiency.

Questions concerning the efficacy of protection in directly improving an industry's fortunes become even more pressing when it is recognized that the indirect negative effects are not adequately taken into account. Conversely, the economic costs of failing to examine indirect effects of protection loom larger if questions arise concerning the sign and magnitude of direct effects.

When consideration is further given to the proposition that using industries that may be harmed by protection are reluctant to protest, economic efficiency may be further diminished when a unanimous industry seeks protection as a perceived means of alleviating its problems. When effective organization and political clout are then important in determining outcomes, there is a further delinking of economic efficiency from the granting of protection.

Add to these considerations concerns as to the "fairness" of the administered protection laws, and it seems clear that questions must be asked about the degree to which current U.S. trade policy achieves objectives that are in the interest of the American people and economic efficiency.

References

Boltuck, Richard, and Robert E. Litan, eds. 1991. *Down in the dumps: Administration of the unfair trade laws.* Washington, D.C.: Brookings Institution.

Isard, Peter. 1973. Employment impacts of textile imports and investment: A vintage-capital model. *American Economic Review* 63, no. 3 (June): 402–16.

Milner, Helen. 1988. *Resisting protectionism: Global industries and the politics of international trade.* Princeton, N.J.: Princeton University Press.

Scherer, F. M. 1992. *International high-technology competition,* 188–89. Cambridge, Mass.: Harvard University Press.

Contributors

J. Michael Finger
The World Bank
Room R2-015
1818 H Street NW
Washington, DC 20433

Bruce L. Gardner
Department of Agricultural Economics
University of Maryland
College Park, MD 20742

Ann Harrison
Graduate School of Business
Columbia University
Office 615 Uris Hall
New York, NY 10027

Douglas A. Irwin
Graduate School of Business
University of Chicago
1101 East 58th Street
Chicago, IL 60637

Joseph P. Kalt
Kennedy School of Government
79 JFK Street
Harvard University
Cambridge, MA 02138

Anne O. Krueger
Department of Economics
Stanford University
Stanford, CA 04305

Michael O. Moore
Department of Economics
George Washington University
Washington, DC 20052

Douglas R. Nelson
Department of Economics
Tilton Hall
Tulane University
New Orleans, LA 70118

David Orden
Virginia Polytechnic Institute and State
    University
Department of Agricultural Economics
Hutcheson Hall
Blacksburg, VA 24061

Robert W. Staiger
Department of Economics
University of Wisconsin
1180 Observatory Drive
Madison, WI 53706

Frank A. Wolak
Department of Economics
Stanford University
Stanford, CA 94305

Author Index

Subject Index